Gay Men, Drinking, and Alcoholism

Thomas S.
Weinberg

SOUTHERN ILLINOIS UNIVERSITY PRESS
Carbondale and Edwardsville

For G. W. Levi Kamel, Ph.D.,

Friend, Colleague, and Collaborator
in Loving Memory

Copyright © 1994 by the Board of Trustees,
        Southern Illinois University
All rights reserved
Printed in the United States of America
Edited by Robin Russell
Design and production supervised by New Leaf Studio

97   96   95   94   4   3   2   1

Library of Congress Cataloging-in-Publication Data

Weinberg, Thomas S.
Gay men, drinking, and alcoholism / Thomas S. Weinberg
    p.   cm.
Includes bibliographical references and index.
1. Gay men—United States—Alcohol use.   I. Title.
HV5139.W45   1994
362.29′22′086642—dc20   93-48387
ISBN 0-8093-1857-1   CIP
ISBN 0-8093-1858-X pbk.

The paper used in this publication meets the minimum
requirements of American National Standard for Information
Sciences—Permanence of Paper for Printed Library Materials,
ANSI Z39.48-1984. ∞

Contents

Tables

Preface

Within the gay community, there is a belief that gays drink heavily and are more likely to suffer the ravages of alcoholism than are members of mainstream society. The National Lesbian and Gay Health Foundation reports that three out of every ten gay people have an alcohol or drug abuse problem (*Buffalo News*, October 30, 1990). No one, however, really knows if this is true. The main source of information on the extent of gay alcohol use and abuse comes from a few surveys done in the mid-1970s. More recent studies have cast some doubt upon the validity of the earlier findings. Casual observation, however, indicates that alcohol use is an integral part of the gay world.

This book is not intended to clear up the question of how many gays have drinking problems. Rather, I am more interested in the nature of drinking, its variations within the gay male community, and adjustments and responses to alcohol use. If, in fact, gays have more problems with alcohol than nongays, the sociological question to be asked is, How does the social organization of the gay world contribute to heavy drinking? Issues that need to be addressed include how social relationships with both friends and lovers affect alcohol use and how the bar and other social settings encourage or discourage drinking.

Sociologists at one time believed that distinctions should be made between the findings of research and their practical application. This is not my perspective. The value of sociological insights lies in their usefulness in solving real-world problems. My primary motivation in undertaking this project was a desire to develop insights that could be used to reduce alcohol problems within the gay community. To that end, I have added a final chapter that builds upon the research in making suggestions I hope will be valuable.

Acknowledgments

The research for this book was supported by a National Institute on Alcohol Abuse and Alcoholism postdoctoral fellowship sponsored by Dr. Jacqueline P. Wiseman. I am grateful to Professor Wiseman for her enthusiastic support, encouragement, and advice, and for her help in obtaining supplementary grants from the Distilled Spirits Council of the United States.

A number of other colleagues encouraged this research by critically reading drafts of several chapters and discussing ideas. Among them are Herbert A. Aurbach, Carl B. Backman, Gene Grabiner, Peter Nardi, Narendra Nath Kalia, and Martha S. Magill. Bonnie A. Beane read several complete drafts of the book, raising important questions. Levi Kamel was a source of ideas, as well as a companion on bar excursions. Although he has passed away, I can still hear his voice in certain phrases and passages in the book.

I am also grateful for the constructive comments and ideas of David Rudy and two anonymous readers for Southern Illinois University Press. I am indebted to Richard D. DeBacher and Curtis L. Clark, editorial directors at SIU Press, for their encouragement. A special thanks is due to Kathy Callanan of the Research Institute on Addictions, who obtained material for me that I could not find elsewhere.

Chapter 5 originally appeared in a shorter and less-developed form as "Love Relationships and Drinking among Gay Men" in the *Journal of Drug Issues*, 16, 637–648. Reprinted with permission.

Gay Men,
Drinking,
and
Alcoholism

1. Gay Men and Drinking: An Introduction

This book is about gay men. It is also about drinking. Alcohol use is one of the most visible behaviors in the gay male world. In fact, drinking is a central aspect of this world, and it plays an important part in the lifestyles of many gay men (Nardi, 1982a; Warren, 1974).

Even though the use of alcoholic beverages is widespread in the gay male community, very little is really known about variation in drinking among gay men and its relationship to the social worlds in which these men move. Few studies have paid even passing attention to this behavior, and fewer still have concentrated specifically on it. Even focused research is normally concerned only with gay alcoholics (e.g., Beaton & Guild, 1976; Small & Leach, 1977) and rarely considers the implications of the social context of alcohol use in the larger gay community.

Most of the extensive body of psychoanalytic literature dating from the early 1900s attempts to locate homosexuality within the etiology of alcoholism (Abraham, 1908/1954; Blum, 1966; Botwinick & Machover, 1951; Fenichel, 1945; Knight, 1937; Machover, Puzzo, Machover, & Plumeau, 1959; McCord & McCord, 1960; Prout, Strongin, & White, 1950; Riggall, 1923). However, there has been no consistent agreement among theorists about the relationship between homosexuality and alcoholism. Some Freudian writers, for example, felt that alcoholics were fixated at the anal stage and that they suffered from repressed homosexuality (Blum, 1966). Other psychoanalysts theorized that alcoholism was linked to homosexual-

1

ity through fixation at the oral stage (Small & Leach, 1977). Still other writers identified compulsive drinking as an attempt to reduce anxiety over one's masculinity, as a means of coping with overidentification with one's father (an indication of latent homosexuality), or as a way of dealing with an irrational fear of heterosexual relationships. The psychoanalytic literature finds no clear-cut, consistent relationship between homosexuality and alcohol abuse and thus sheds little light on alcohol use among gay men. It focuses only on alcoholism, rather than on drinking behavior in general, and its findings are, at best, contradictory and confusing.

Survey research, although very sparse, is an improvement on the psychoanalytic tradition because it attempts to make some observations about drinking in general within the gay community. However, these studies vary widely, not only in methodological rigor and sophistication, but also in their findings. Despite claims that "research indicates that approximately one out of three gay male adults in metropolitan areas abuse or are dependent on alcohol" (Icard & Traunstein, 1987, p. 267), the extent of gay alcoholism or problem drinking is not all that clear. This estimate can be traced back to research done in the mid-1970s to the late 1970s that suffered from the lack of a clear definition of alcoholism and problem drinking and had numerous methodological difficulties (Fifield, 1975; Fifield, Lathan, & Phillips, 1977; Lohrenz, Connelly, Coyne, & Spare, 1978).[1] In my view, this research has been cited uncritically so often that it has become part of the mythology of gay alcohol studies, in much the same way that Kinsey's estimate that 10% of the population is gay has become, until quite recently, an unchallenged truth (Barringer, 1993; Rogers, 1993).

In a more recent, carefully designed comparative study, Stall and Wiley (1988) note that, while approximately 75% of gay males are frequent drinkers, only about 19% of them are frequent and heavy alcohol users,[2] and this figure probably includes men who are not alcoholics or problem drinkers. They conclude that "the existence of exceptionally high prevalence rates (i.e., 30%) for alcoholism and/or problem drinking, as previously reported in the literature, could not be inferred from the data presented here" (p. 70). Stall and Wiley call for "participant observation study of the social settings in which gay drug and alcohol use occurs as well as the consequences of such use," which they feel would "provide valuable ethnographic insights to help interpret the epidemiological survey data" (p. 71).

Only very superficial ethnographic attention has been paid by researchers to normal drinking behavior among gay men, such as how sexual contacts are made in bars. These studies have rarely been guided by any systematic theoretical framework (e.g., Achilles, 1967; Cavan, 1966; Delph, 1978; Hooker, 1967; Read, 1980; Warren, 1974). Warren's book is really the only ethnographic study that even attempts to explain the social meaning of alcohol use for gay men. Her work, however, was a general study of one upper-middle-class gay community and did not focus primarily on drinking. The other observational studies, all of which examined behavior in bars, had almost nothing to say about actual drinking, and they also failed to show the relevance of other behavior, such as socializing and "cruising" (i.e., making sexual contacts), to alcohol use.

A few case studies of gay alcoholics have been published (Beaton & Guild, 1976; Colcher, 1982; Small & Leach, 1977). They are important but have been written from a counseling viewpoint, rather than from the academic perspective of social science. Some of their contributions and those of others dealing with therapeutic interventions with gay problem drinkers will be discussed in chapter 10. Besides the professional literature, a few authoritative articles for the gay layman (e.g., Shilts, 1976) have appeared in the gay press.

Thus, there is a large gap in the literature concerning gay drinking, even in such a highly alcohol-specific setting as a bar. And there certainly is a need to look at other aspects of the gay world as they are related to alcohol consumption. For example, to my knowledge no one has documented the part alcohol plays in the everyday lives of gay men, the ways love relationships affect and are affected by drinking, the ways in which members of the gay community respond to heavy drinking and alcohol-related problems, and the influence of friends on drinking and bar visitation patterns. The ethnographic literature consists of studies that are primarily observational and that make only infrequent use of systematically gathered in-depth interview materials, so that often what is presented is the researcher's point of view, rather than the meanings his or her respondents place on their own and others' behavior.

The survey research and the psychoanalytic literature present other problems. They are often plagued with difficulties stemming from preconceived notions about the nature and extent of pathological drinking. The psychoanalytic literature, in particular, is replete with value judgments and, of course, focuses only on "alcoholics."

Recently, writers have begun to develop theoretical formulations to explain gay alcoholism. Nardi (1982a, 1982b), for example, has examined some of the unique characteristics of the gay world, such as the special importance of nontraditional family structures for gays, and their implications for excessive drinking. Although his own writing lacks a concrete data base, Nardi's insights are nevertheless quite valuable, and have helped to explain many of the observations made in the present study. In an almost psychoanalytical vein (i.e., using the Freudian mechanism of suppressed reaction formation), Kus (1988) linked alcoholism with nonacceptance of one's gay self, holding that "it is the internalized homophobia prior to having reached the stage of Acceptance in the coming out process which is the root of alcoholism of gay men" (p. 27). McKirnan and Peterson (1988, 1989) developed a sophisticated stress-vulnerability model, which looks at the interaction of stress factors such as discrimination (stigmatization, verbal harassment, employment difficulties, assault) and negative affectivity (moderate depression, low self-esteem, alienation) with vulnerabilities such as expectancies that alcohol can lower tension and cultural learning about the availability and social role of alcohol, including using bars as a social resource. As instructive as these formulations may be, however, they still ignore the wider range of drinking patterns and adjustments within the social worlds of gay men.

The Perspective of This Book

The present study is intended to fill the gaps detailed above in the literature concerning gay male drinking. It was designed to examine gay male drinking in a broader social context, to discover the meanings embedded in its use, and to describe the role drinking plays within the gay male subculture. The framework for analysis is symbolic interactionism, which focuses on

> the individual "with a self" and on the interaction between a person's internal thoughts and emotions and his or her social behavior. . . . Individuals are viewed as active constructors of their own conduct

who interpret, evaluate, define, and map out their own action, rather than as passive beings who are impinged upon by outside forces. Symbolic interactionism also stresses the processes by which the individual makes decisions and forms opinions. (Wallace & Wolf, 1991, p. 237)

My emphasis is placed on drinking as social behavior, focusing on the influence of social context (e.g., the expectations of bar patrons and love relationships) on individual drinking patterns.

The most viable explanation for drinking among gay men, for which evidence is presented in this book, is based upon reference group theory. Human behavior is not haphazard, nor is it driven simply by biological imperatives. It is guided by norms, values, and expectations, learned within a group context, which define group membership and one's relationships with others.

The power of groups to define and influence behavior is well known. Many writers have emphasized the importance of integration into groups as a determinant of behavior. The extent to which an individual is integrated into a group, identifies with the group, and develops a commitment to the group and its values will affect many aspects of behavior. The nature of specific norms and expectations, their clarity, whether they are proscriptive or prescriptive (Mizruchi & Perrucci, 1962), the ways they are related to other aspects of group life, and whether other competing definitions of acceptable behavior are present, all affect how people behave.

As Charon (1985) notes, in order to understand an individual's behavior, "we must . . . begin to understand how one defines the situation, the reference group one identifies with in that situation, the perspective one draws on, and how one's role, reference groups, and/or perspectives undergo change in the situation in interaction with others" (p. 25). This approach has the advantage of directing attention to the perspective of the drinkers themselves and, accordingly, to the meanings these men place on their own and others' drinking behavior. I take a social worlds approach here (Glassner & Loughlin, 1987; Greenberg, 1988), presenting my respondents' situation as they see it by allowing them to speak in their own voices.

Although I devote much space to an examination of alcoholics and problem drinkers, this is not a book just about alcoholism. It is a book about drinking, which means that I am concerned with the variety of drinking adjustments among gay men, including those who are infrequent, light, and moderate drinkers. The model of drinking involvement developed in this study examines the ways in which the social relationships of gay men account for their different drinking patterns. For example, heavier drinkers tend to socialize with others who consume large amounts of alcohol, attend parties where drinking is prevalent, and spend a good deal of time in the bars. Lighter drinkers are usually involved with men for whom drinking is not an important activity; they tend to meet people in nondrinking contexts and to be actively involved in the gay community outside of the bar scene. The norms, attitudes, and values of the various social worlds in which men participate are stronger determinants of their drinking behavior than factors such as discrimination, alienation, and stress, although the latter can trigger short-term heavy drinking. As a man moves from one social context to another, from one situation to the next, his drinking behavior can and does change.

The Plan of This Book

Chapter 2 is a discussion of the research methods of the study. It outlines the procedures used in data collection, describes the characteristics of the respondents, and discusses the gay subculture of "Paradise City," the fictitious name used in this study for the West Coast city in which the research was carried out.

Chapter 3 examines drinking as social behavior in the gay male subculture. I identify drinking as being intimately entwined with friendship networks and extended families in the gay world. I then look at the settings in which the men in the study drink, and pay special attention to the situations that they say cause them to increase or decrease their alcohol consumption. In addition, the chapter presents the men's perceptions of their friends' drinking and the ways in which they and their friends respond to excessive alcohol use.

Chapter 4 explores the gay bar scene, discussing the importance of the bar in gay life, the process of entering the bar subculture, interaction within the bar as it relates to drinking, and the interrelations among friendship groups, the expectations of bar patrons, and alcohol consumption. Inducements to drinking used by the bar management and the role of the bartender are also examined. Finally, I look at those factors related to leaving the bar world.

Chapter 5 focuses on love relationships and drinking. A general discussion of drinking among gay couples is presented, followed by a more specific examination of the effect of love relationships on drinking, including those circumstances that tend to increase and decrease alcohol consumption for couples. Then, I turn to a discussion of the effects of drinking on love relationships and the ways in which the men in the study dealt with heavily drinking lovers.

Chapter 6 is concerned with the drinking careers of the men in the sample. Among the issues examined are the nature of their early experiences with alcohol, their reasons for using alcohol, and their feelings when drinking. In addition, the men's feelings about drinking, their periods of abstinence, and the responses of others to these periods are illustrated. I focus on the respondents' feelings, worries, and concerns about drinking; any problems they may have had with alcohol; the way they dealt with these problems; the reactions of others to these problems; and the men's attempts to correct them. I also look at such factors as the men's perceptions of parental and sibling alcohol use.

Chapter 7 examines those men who are infrequent, light, or moderate drinkers. Their early and current drinking behavior is compared. I identify the factors that are related to their less frequent use of alcohol, such as their social relationships, their organizational affiliations, the drinking behavior of their friends, and the contexts in which they drink.

Chapter 8 looks more closely at those men who have defined themselves as alcoholics or problem drinkers and discusses how they came to label themselves in these ways, what they did about their drinking, and what the reactions of significant others were. Special attention is paid to abstinence and relapse cycles and to turning points in their drinking careers.

Chapter 9 considers three alternative explanations for gay problem drinking: the alienation thesis, the influence of parental problem drinking, and reference group theory. This chapter departs from the predominantly ethnographic descriptions of earlier chapters by including statistical correlation techniques to uncover the relationships between heavy alcohol use, problem drinking, and a variety of other variables.

Chapter 10 examines strategies for reducing gay problem drinking. Gay drinking is placed in perspective by examining the similarities and differences between alcohol use in the homosexual and heterosexual communities. Gay drinking is discussed as a special situation, and a processual model of gay problem drinking is developed, utilizing the interviews with respondents, participant observation, and correlation analysis. Based on this model and the available literature on therapeutic intervention, recommendations are made for reducing alcohol abuse in the gay male community.

2. Research Methods

Since I wished to understand the social meaning of alcohol use for gay men and the ways in which the gay community responds to drinking, I chose ethnographic techniques—participant observation combined with in-depth interviewing—as the most appropriate ways to gather data. Because my intention is to give the reader an understanding of drinking patterns from within the gay community, my strategy in this book is to highlight the attitudes, feelings, and perspectives of the men I interviewed, in their own voices. As Nardi (1991) writes, "If one focuses on the social context in which gay people find themselves, how they define reality and perceive their situation, and what symbols and values they hold with respect to alcohol use, one begins to develop a more complete picture of the relationship between homosexuality and alcoholism" (p. 297). Recognizing that there is not necessarily a one-to-one relationship between the perspective of ethnographers and that of the populations they study, I have kept my own descriptions to a minimum, using them primarily as a supplement to the interviews.

Entering the Field

When I first arrived in Paradise City,[1] I knew few people there. Although I had no contacts in that gay community, I was familiar with the gay subculture in other places. My initial problem was to familiarize myself with the setting, learn where bars and other gay institutions were located, and begin to establish relationships with people in the community. I needed to be able to participate not only in the easily accessible public gay institutions but also in more intimate social networks. I intended to gather data using in-depth interviews, and my interpretation of these data would be more credible if based on a personal understanding of the contexts and situations referred to by respondents. Because I needed an orientation to the community, I wanted to introduce myself to some of the people who would be most knowledgeable and whose support and cooperation would be helpful. My first step was to call the Gay Center and make an appointment to meet the director.

The Gay Center was located at that time in a yellow two-story frame building in the "Loma de Oro" section of Paradise City. As I climbed the stairs to the director's office, I had some concerns about how I would be received. Researchers are often viewed as voyeurs and exploiters, a perspective that is not totally inaccurate. Although my interest in the issue of gay drinking and alcoholism was sincere, I could not be sure that it would be perceived that way by others.

Once I met Bob, a large and affable man, my fears were put to rest. We felt comfortable with each other immediately. He asked questions about my academic and personal background and was very enthusiastic and supportive. His ongoing encouragement of my research facilitated my making contacts in the community, developing friendship networks, and learning about the local gay scenes and institutions. Bob was starting a men's support group and suggested that I join. He thought that it would be a good way to meet people and to learn about the issues that were important to gays in Paradise City.

The following week I went to Bob's house for the first meeting of the group. There were six others besides Bob and me. We sat around in a circle, and Bob asked us to introduce ourselves and explain why we were there. When it was my turn, I told the others that I had recently come to Paradise City. As the other men had done, I talked a bit about my personal background. I mentioned that I was a sociologist and that I was interested in the issue of drinking among gay men, but I did not emphasize the point. The men accepted my information in a matter-of-fact way.

We met once a week, with each of us taking turns hosting the group in our homes. I remained in the group as long as it existed, which was almost two years. During that period the composition of the group changed as some members left and others took their places. The group varied from about six to a dozen members at any given time. The contacts I made through the support group

developed into close friendships with several of the men, especially Sully, Phil, and Hal. We spent a great deal of time together,
socializing, attending events, and going out to the bars. All of them
knew of my research project, and some of them volunteered to
participate in the formal interviews. Gradually, I expanded my participation to a variety of drinking-related situations such as bars,
private parties, dinner parties, potluck dinners, restaurants, beach
parties, and picnics, not only through friendships made in the support group, but also with men like Steven, whom I met as a result
of the interviews.

Although at one time or another I visited almost all of the gay
bars in Paradise City, most of my observations were confined to
about a dozen of them, which were representative of small and large
dance bars, conversation bars, denim and leather bars, neighborhood
taverns, and piano bars. To a great extent, my choices reflected the
interests of my friends. For example, if I went out with Hal, we
would most often frequent the Sultan or occasionally Her Place, a
lesbian bar where Hal had friends. Sully, Phil, and I would go to
the Sultan or the Pacific Coast or sometimes Gunsmoke. Lee favored
the leather bars, so we spent time in the Dungeon, the Docks, and
J.B.'s. Once in a while, several of us would go to the Brass Monkey,
a dance bar that has existed over twenty years. After the bars closed
for the night, some of us might go to one of several popular restaurants for coffee. Normally, we would encounter some of the men
whom we had seen out that night.

After two years spent continuously in the field, I left Paradise
City. For the third and subsequent five years, I returned twice
annually, in December and during the summer months, for periods
ranging from two to eight weeks. By so doing, I maintained contacts
in the community, and I have been able to note changes in Paradise
City's gay world.

Interviews

The core of my data comes from in-depth, taped interviews,
from one-and-a-half to three hours long, guided by an interview
schedule.[2] Five respondents who participated in these interviews
were members of the men's support group. Others were found by
placing advertisements in local newspapers and gay publications.
The advertisements read:

GAY MEN INTERESTED in responding to a questionnaire on personal drinking patterns please contact Dr. Tom Weinberg, Sociology Department, Western State University, or call 555-2222.

Thirty-three men responded to this advertisement. My contacts were also expanded through snowball techniques; previous respondents were asked to recommend other potential participants in the study. Eight additional respondents were obtained in this way, of whom five were referred to me by one man.

When contacted by a potential respondent, I spent some time on the phone explaining the study, asking screening questions, and setting up an appointment. Most commonly, men would ask me what kind of doctor I was and what the study was about. I usually gave them a brief synopsis of my interests, telling them that my goal was to understand the place of alcohol in the gay community, so that ways might be found to help those with problems. Sometimes a man would volunteer that he was only a light or occasional drinker and that he thought he might have little to add to my project. In those cases, I explained that I was not just interested in heavy or problem drinkers, but that I needed to understand the wide range of drinking patterns and adjustments in the gay community. Usually, the potential respondent was reassured that he could help.

I screened callers for age, since I did not want to interview anyone under eighteen. I also asked how long they had been "out" and whether they went to the bars. A few times I suspected that the callers were not gay and had ulterior motives for contacting me because their responses indicated that they were ignorant about homosexuality and the Paradise City gay scene. In those cases, I quickly terminated the conversation.

Interviews were arranged to take place either at my office at the university or in a respondent's home. Occasionally, other settings, such as an outdoor shopping mall or a park, were sites for interviews. At the initial call, I obtained the man's phone number and called him on the day before the interview to remind him of our appointment. This was important because it was not unusual for a man to forget and to miss an appointment. Patrick, for example, was not home for our scheduled appointment. When I called to reschedule, he claimed he had forgotten. The second time I went to see him, he was not home either. I drove around for awhile, then called from a public telephone. He asked me to come right over. When I arrived there, I found two neighbors visiting with him. He had also brought home a young man whom he had picked up at the Dungeon. Once the neighbors had left, I asked Patrick if he wished to reschedule the interview, as it seemed to me that he really did not want to be interviewed. He insisted that we go ahead. Patrick had obviously been drinking heavily, and he asked me, in a hostile tone, whether I was writing a "term paper." I told him I was a professional sociologist who had done extensive research in the gay community and that this interview was not for a term paper. At first, his answers to my questions were terse, but gradually he relaxed, and by the end of the interview, he was actively chatting away. Apparently, I had somehow won him over.

Characteristics of the Respondents

During my time in the field, I formally interviewed forty-six gay men. Their median age was twenty-nine years (with a range of twenty-one to sixty-eight years). The respondents were drawn from a wide range of occupational, educational, and income categories. Twenty-five men were Protestant, seventeen men were Catholic, two were Jewish, one respondent was Mormon, and one was a nondenominational Christian. The ethnic background of the men was predominantly northwestern European (see table 1).

The men displayed a variety of drinking adjustments and patterns, yet almost two-thirds of them were moderately heavy to heavy drinkers.[3] The only abstainers were six men who identified themselves as recovering alcoholics (four other self-avowed alcoholics were still drinking). Too much should not be made of this finding, however. The preponderance of heavier drinkers in the study may simply be a function of how the data were collected, since men with drinking problems may have been more likely to respond to advertisements in a conscious or only vaguely conceived attempt to get some help. There is also a possible bias built into using referral chains, since men do tend to drink the way their friends do. This does not seem to be a terribly important distortion, however, because only eight men came from referrals and the respondents referred to me by men I had already interviewed only generally reflected the drinking patterns of their friends. For example, one respondent, Steven, who later became a close friend and a staunch supporter of

*Table 1.   Demographic Characteristics of Respondents
(in percentage)*

Age				
21–30	31–40	41–50	51+	
56	28	7	9	

Education				
some h.s.	h.s. grad.	some coll.	coll. grad.	grad. school
2	13	36	29	20

Occupation				
unempl	studn	unskl	skil/cler	manag/profes
5	11	11	27	46

Income				
under $5K	$5K–14.9K	$15K–24.9K	$25K–34.9K	$35K+
14	44	26	7	7

Lived in Paradise City				
under 1 year	1–5	6–10	11–20	20+
13	28	17	20	22

my research, was a moderately heavy drinker. Of the five men whom he referred to me, however, only one was also a moderately heavy drinker, one was a light drinker, and three were moderate consumers of alcohol. A second man, who was himself a heavy drinker, referred two friends, only one of whom was also a heavy drinker. The five members of the men's support group were all moderately heavy drinkers. It is important to remember that I was not interested in the proportions of various types of drinkers in the gay male community but in the variety of drinking arrangements and adjustments.

The Gay Subculture of Paradise City

Paradise City is one of the fastest growing areas in the United States. Part of the reason for this rapid population increase is Paradise City's mild climate. Blessed with miles of beaches, beautiful parks, and desert and mountain recreation areas, Paradise City draws thousands of tourists as well as more permanent migrants every year. In 1980, the city's population was almost 900,000, an increase of about 37% over that of 1970. By 1990, it had expanded to 1,094,524. This puts Paradise City among the top dozen U.S. cities in size. An additional million people inhabit the rest of "Paradise County."

Among the many recent settlers in Paradise City are large numbers of gay people. Very few of the men interviewed for this study were Paradise City natives, and not many more were born in "Western State." Although some men had lived in Paradise City for as long as twenty years, most respondents were relative newcomers. Gay spokespersons have estimated that there are between 95,000 and 125,000 gays living in Paradise County.

Gay Areas

While gay people live throughout Paradise City and Paradise County, there are a few areas of residence within which they are highly concentrated. The best known gay area is "Las Cumbres." A number of gay-run businesses, gay bars, and private clubs, and at least one gay-oriented theater are all located there. At least one bathhouse has recently opened, a trend which also can be found in other cities, despite the continuing AIDS crisis.

Las Cumbres borders the downtown district and City Park, the site of cruising areas and tearooms, public restrooms in which men have impersonal sex (see Humphreys, 1970). Life in Las Cumbres is described by a former resident in the following way:

> There's a community in Paradise City [in which] just about everyone who lives in the neighborhood is gay. They live in the gay community and when I say gay community, I'm talking about living and working, socializing, just your complete life in a gay atmosphere. . . .
>
> Las Cumbres is very heavily gay populated. I mean, I can drive through Las Cumbres and I can see—maybe there's a hundred people on the street—I have seen seventy-five of them before. That's how strong it is. And the people who want to become totally involved with the gay lifestyle, I think that's where they all migrate to at one time or another. I guess they feel more relaxed. They can walk down the street with each other; they can dress how they want to, you know, and people up there have been exposed more so to the gay world than let's say someone who lives in [the suburbs]. They feel more comfortable there. (Mark)

Two other areas of gay residence, bordering each other and Las Cumbres, are "Loma de Oro" and "Del Parque." Loma de Oro is, in large part, a lower socioeconomic area. Gays are concentrated only in a small portion of the area, close to the downtown and Las Cumbres areas on one side, and the Del Parque area on the other. In the past, the Gay Center had been located in Loma de Oro. It has since moved to the Del Parque area.

Del Parque is not just a residential community for gays, but, like Las Cumbres, it also contains a number of gay institutions. In addition to the Gay Center, several gay bars, a Metropolitan Community Church,[4] a physical fitness center catering to gay men, and a number of restaurants known to attract a gay clientele are found in Del Parque.

Ocean View is a beach community that has both a gay bathhouse and a gay hotel. However, it is not an important gay residential area.

Gay Organizations and Institutions

The gay community in Paradise City is very active and vocal. It communicates through two local gay newspapers, which contain news of upcoming special events such as the Gay Pride Parade, the Mr. Nude Paradise City Contest, and the Hookers' and Hustlers' Ball; court actions relevant to the gay community; national and international incidents relevant to the gay community; stories about and interviews with nationally known and local gay celebrities and institutions; advice columns, letters to the editor, reviews of movies, plays, and books; advertisements for gay bars, hotels, spas, bathhouses, and other businesses. Paradise City also has its own magazine, and posters and advertisements for upcoming events are displayed in its numerous gay bars.[5]

Many clubs and organizations cater to gay people with special interests including Wilderness Explorers, Gay Gourmets, Gay Fathers, a soccer club, a volleyball team, bicycling clubs, organizations for older gay men and lesbians, support groups, and so forth. In addition, a gay repertory company performs in a theater near the Old Town area of the city. A recently purchased and renovated building housing the Metropolitan Community Church is located in Del Parque, and another is in North Paradise County. There is the Lesbian and Gay Center as well as a halfway house for gay and lesbian alcoholics. Several Gay Alcoholics Anonymous (AA) meetings are scattered throughout Paradise County. A residential facility for AIDS patients is in North Paradise County.

Through a number of voluntary associations and organizations including three political clubs and a political action committee, the gay community has been able to influence the existing political structure. Politicians are endorsed by the gay community, and law enforcement has made some concessions to it. For example, I attended a luncheon of the Greater Paradise City Business Association (an organization of gay and lesbian business and professional leaders) at which the guest of honor was the chief of police. In response to questions about enforcement policy and a recent incident in which gay transvestites had been arrested for impersonating females, the tone of the chief's response was apologetic and conciliatory. Recently, the police department has instituted a liaison officer to work with the gay community. In the aftermath of at least thirty-five attacks on people in the Las Cumbres and Del Parque areas, which included the fatal beating of a teenager by alleged skinheads during the second half of 1991, the police department set up a special task force and also trained citizen volunteers who have been patrolling these areas.

While the gay organizations and institutions discussed above are important features of gay life in Paradise City, the intimate social relationships that people form are much more important to them. Understanding the nature of friendship networks, or what Nardi (1982a) has called extended families, is critical in placing the drinking behavior of gay men in the proper social context.

3. Drinking as Social Behavior

Friendship Networks and Extended Families

A fundamental, critical difference between homosexuals and heterosexuals is that for gay people, the development of sexual identity is problematic. Almost always, the child or adolescent who eventually acquires a gay identity becomes painfully aware that he or she is somehow different from his or her peers (Dank, 1971; Troiden, 1979; Weinberg, 1983). Often the individuals are not clear about the nature of this difference, and they feel alone and isolated and must figure out what is going on without any help.

When they first decided that they were definitely gay, half of the men I interviewed felt frightened, "not very good," or confused.

> TOM: How did you feel about being gay at that time?

> SULLY: I think most of the time I felt like, "Oh, God, I'm the only person on earth like this." Because I didn't know any gay people at that time.

> DANIEL: I attempted suicide at that time. I felt very badly. I felt that I was really abnormal.

> NORMAN: It was very frightening. You feel like you're the only one, you know. And you've got this whole world out there to fight.

In an attempt to understand himself and his feelings, the individual often seeks out other gay people (Dank, 1971; Troiden, 1979;

Weinberg, 1983). These people facilitate his development of identity by enabling him to feel more comfortable in all-gay settings than he does when he is with heterosexuals, by serving as positive role models, by sharing their own past histories and experiences with him, and by enabling him to develop gay pride (Weinberg, 1983). These others may now become part of a network of friends, an extended family (Nardi, 1982a). Since gays are sometimes estranged from their families of origin, either because they feel rejected or because they wish to maintain their privacy, friends become especially important as role models, reference groups, and sources of psychological and material support.

> TOM: Where does your family live?
> PETER: My biological family?
> TOM: Yes.
> PETER: New York.
> TOM: Do you have another kind of family?
> PETER: Yeah, I belong to a real community that I sort of see as a family. Basically, the gay community. In a lot of ways, [it] feels like home. The Gay Center, specifically. . . . Like, for example, when I just moved, everybody who helped me, except [one person] was connected with the Center. It was a real discovery that there's this support network there for me.

Many gay people spend holidays and celebrate important occasions with a special circle of close friends, rather than with their blood relations. Thus, the attitudes, interests, and activities of friends become relevant for gay people in ways they do not for single heterosexuals. The extended family structure builds in an intimacy and a wider range of concerns that seem to be lacking in heterosexual friendships, and the influence of friends' behavior is consequently magnified. Nardi (1982a) explains the special importance of friendship networks for gay people:

> The gay experience in a heterosexual world also leads to the formation of a network of close friends who aid in the development and maintenance of gay identity. Unlike a group of close heterosexual friends for the heterosexual, this gay "extended family" arises out of a need to find role models and identity in an oppressive society. . . . In this context, it becomes an intense friendship group contributing importantly to gay identity formation and maintenance. How

members of the "extended family" define drinking practices and evaluate drunkenness will have an impact on a person's problem drinking behavior and recovery. (p. 86)

To understand alcohol use among gay men, it is necessary to look at the importance of social relationships for gay people because they strongly influence not only drinking but other sorts of behavior as well. The men tended to drink the way their friends drank, so that those respondents whose circle included heavy drinkers were themselves avid consumers of alcohol.[1]

Warren (1974) has pointed out that alcohol is an indispensable accompaniment of gay social life, and this is apparent in statements made by many of the men in this study. They noted that most of their drinking occurred in social situations, and that their consumption was a response to that of their friends.

> Tom: In what situations do you usually use alcohol?
> Chuck: [On my] days off and just to party with people. All my friends and everyone I know, just about, drink.

Friends often influenced drinking both in terms of making decisions about visiting drinking-related settings and in creating an atmosphere conducive to alcohol consumption. For example, one's friends might define a situation as a party, thus making it difficult to get into the appropriate spirit or mood without consuming alcohol.

> Tom: In what settings would you say most of your alcohol drinking takes place?
> Gary: Well, now it's at parties, where everybody's drinking, especially if there is a keg. I don't want to feel left out of anything.

The interaction of friends, drinking, and social life was probably best summarized by Mark, who explained the place of alcohol in the gay subculture in the following way:

> Social life is really limited in the gay world to where, when you go to someplace socially in public, you don't really have a choice. There's always alcohol there and that's what everyone is partaking of. I suppose I wouldn't have to, but it just becomes a way of life after awhile. I would say that 90% of the gay people . . . I know who have a social life drink three or four days a week.

Mark's experience illustrates the finding that for almost all of the men, drinking was social behavior. Only three men reported that they usually drank alone.[2] Other men also addressed the interrelations between friends' expectations and drinking. For example, in explaining why his drinking had decreased, Gary said that his visits to bars had become infrequent. "I think one reason why I don't go to the bars anymore is because my friends don't go out either." His friends reduced their own bar visits because they had become involved in love relationships, were finishing school, or had decided that they were not sexually successful in bar settings.

Mark noted that at one point he began to feel that he was drinking too much. In order to control his drinking, he moved away from the predominantly gay area in which he was living and changed jobs and friends. "That solved a lot of problems," he said. He reduced his alcohol consumption by seeking out other people whose social life did not include heavy drinking.

Drinking Settings and Situations

Although the men in the study drank in a variety of settings and situations, the largest proportion of them (41%) identified the gay bar as the setting in which most of their drinking took place. Seventy-four percent of my respondents went to bars at least once a month. This is a much higher proportion than that reported in most studies of monthly bar attendance by heterosexuals (e.g., Cosper, Okraku, & Neumann, 1987; Fisher, 1981). Kraft (1981) is an exception. Sixty-four percent of his college students reported at least monthly bar visits. The bar scene is so central to gay life that I have devoted chapter 4 to its examination.

Parties and Dinners

In the course of her research, Warren (1974) attended numerous private functions that she classified as home entertainments, cocktail parties, and spectaculars, depending on how elaborate they were, how many people were in attendance, if formal invitations had been used, and whether or not entertainment was provided. She described the place of alcohol in home entertaining in the following way:

> In gay home sociability, a bargain is struck between hosts and guests.
> The hosts' obligation is to provide the liquor that will enable the
> guests to relax and engage in conversation; the guests' obligation is
> to do so, and to do so in a proper manner. . . . Liquor is a necessary
> element in making such entertainment "go," and the host, ensuring
> sociable conversation by his fulfillment of his obligation, never leaves
> a cocktail or wine glass (with dinner) empty throughout the evening.
> "Go," in fact, is partly dependent on the attainment of a degree of
> intoxication among the guests, as well as on the correct number of
> people. (pp. 46, 50)

This bargain described by Warren is so important to gay sociability that even most "dry" households feel an obligation to have alcohol
present on social occasions for nonabstainers. Some men feel offended if they are not offered alcoholic beverages when they go to
someone's home. "I expect to be offered a drink when I go visiting,"
Bill told me. "I hate to go visiting and not even be offered a drink.
I may refuse the drink, but I at least expect to be offered one. If
somebody doesn't want to offer me a drink—I just feel that they
don't know how to entertain."

Parties, especially, as the men have indicated above, are defined
as occasions on which alcohol consumption is necessary to fit in.
Although only two men said that most of their alcohol use occurred
during parties, these situations are the second most frequently mentioned (by 52% of the men) context during which drinking is expected
behavior. This is a much smaller proportion than that found by Kraft
(1981) in his study of college students. Ninety percent of Kraft's
respondents went to parties at least once a month where alcohol
was served (including 45% who attended two to five parties a month
and 15% who attended six or more during that time period), and
83% of them drank at those parties. For students, parties are more
important settings for drinking than are bars, pubs, or taverns. For
the gay men in the present study, the reverse is true.

Clark (1981) has pointed out that the literature on drinking contexts shows that "as far as drinking 'larger than usual amounts' is
concerned, it is apparently the party and not the tavern that looms
largest" (p. 8). This was not true for the gay men with whom I spoke.
Only seven men noted that their heaviest drinking occurred during
such events. Their drinking increased, they said, because they felt
comfortable, relaxed, and unpressured in a party situation. They

were not there to make sexual contacts or to impress anyone. Drinking in a bar, Rodney noted, is "more related to the awkwardness of the situation, [while] if I go to a party, it's more social, and I can actually enjoy drinking more." Sully said that he increased his alcohol consumption at parties where he knew most of the people because "I'm more comfortable. I guess what I'm saying is that I don't have to maintain any certain image or anything." And Bob felt that he would drink more at parties in his own home because he would "feel safe and secure." He said, additionally: "I'm usually very jolly that people were here, so I would just kind of automatically participate. Probably without paying a hell of a lot of attention to it. And my drinking would escalate if I were using pot at the same time that the social [activity was] also happening. . . ." Bob's remarks illustrate what Warren (1974) meant by "normal trouble" in the gay community. Excessive drinking, which can be explained by being "carried away by the extremes of sociability," occurs only in groups, she wrote, and is not defined as alcoholism by gays (pp. 58–59). From my observations at numerous gay parties and social events, heavy drinking, when it occurred, and untoward behavior such as the overly amorous advances that sometimes accompanied it, were usually ignored, except when someone would arrange for the individual's transportation home. Generally, the evening's behavior was not a topic for later conversation:

> We were over at Bob's house for a potluck dinner. About thirty men showed up during the course of the evening, although a core of a dozen or so men remained the entire time. By about 11:00, several partygoers were very drunk. One man continually kept making passes at the others, fondling and trying to kiss them. He was gently but firmly ignored.
>
> Around midnight, Jim and a friend decided to go home. They were so intoxicated that they could barely stand up; they were hanging onto each other and staggering around. No one seemed particularly concerned, although a few people offered them rides. When they said that they would walk home, this arrangement was accepted. No one expressed further interest.
>
> No mention was subsequently made of the events of that night.

In contrast with the situation described above, some of my friends have on several occasions voiced concern over the drinking behavior of others who got drunk on every occasion of sociability, who drank at inappropriate times or in nonsocial settings, and whose consequent behavior was described as obnoxious (see Warren, 1974).

> Sully and I had planned to go out to the bars. Since it was still early, we sat around his apartment, drinking coffee and waiting for Phil to show up. I asked Sully about some of our friends, most of whom had been members of the men's support group. I hadn't seen them for awhile, because I'd been back East for several months. "I'm worried about P. J., Tom," Sully said. "Every time I see him out he's drunk. Hal's noticed the same thing. He drinks too much." I said that I thought P. J. usually held his liquor well. "Not any more," Sully told me. "He's always smashed nowadays." "Has anyone talked to him about it?" I asked. "No, Tom. He'd just get pissed off. He doesn't care."

Although concern with others' drinking was sometimes expressed, it was rare for friends to have actually confronted the men whom they saw as problem drinkers. Instead, they were more likely to simply avoid people whose drinking was unacceptable. Bill, for example, reported that "some of the friends we have drink a lot, but I find that someone who drinks a lot eventually ends up on the outside, as far as I'm concerned." Since Bill is himself a moderately heavy drinker,[3] it is apparent that excessive alcohol consumption is a relative matter.[4]

Home Drinking

According to Clark's (1981) review of studies of public drinking contexts, "the place where most drinkers most often drink is at home" (p. 8). This was not true for the gay men in this study. Just slightly more than one-third of the men indicated that most of their drinking took place in their own homes. Two men said that they divided their drinking evenly between home and the bar. One of them explained that he drank during the evening: if he came directly home from work he would drink there, but if he stopped at a bar or if his roommate urged him to go out, drinking would take place outside the home. The six recovering alcoholics had evenly divided their drinking between home and the bar.

Clark (1981) makes another observation: "Interestingly, relatively more heavy drinkers than light drinkers report that home is the most frequent place of drinking" (p. 8). This was, in fact, true for the gay men. Not counting the past behavior of the recovering alcoholics, more than twice as many moderately heavy and heavy drinkers than light or moderate drinkers reported drinking primarily at home. This is not particularly surprising, since many heavy and problem drinkers tend to isolate themselves when drinking and are not concerned with the social aspects of alcohol use.

One man, a moderately heavy drinker, made an interesting distinction between the context of his most frequent alcohol use and that of his heavy "destructive" drinking.

> TOM: In what settings would you say most of your drinking takes place nowadays?
>
> GREGORY: My heavy drinking is [all] done in bars . . . [but] I'd say that in terms of just drinking an alcoholic beverage, because I'm not going out as often as other times in my life, I'm drinking more at home. Or in other people's homes. But as far as what I consider alcoholic or destructive type drinking—and I don't think it necessarily has to end in a scene or anything to be destructive—but what I think of as negative as opposed to, you know, just pleasant drinking, occurs almost solely in the bars.

Drinking in the homes of friends on occasions other than parties was reported by 52% of the men. Of these men, 25% said this occurred frequently, 42% said this happened sometimes, and 33% said they and their friends drank only rarely at each other's homes. When the men were asked, Do you drink more or less on these occasions (when you are visiting friends but not having a party) than you do at the bars or in some public setting?, 36% said that they drank more, 46% replied that they drank about the same, and 18% said that they drank less.

Situations Causing Increases and Decreases in Drinking

Obviously, for the gay men in the study, as for most people, drinking was a social activity, and their increases and decreases in alcohol consumption were intimately intertwined with the use of alcohol by others. In fact, over one-third of the men made it clear that they were consciously aware of adjusting their alcohol use to conform to what others were doing in a particular setting. Some of them said they would occasionally drink more than they normally would because the people around them were drinking heavily:

> With certain friends I would tend to drink more. . . . It's almost as if not drinking is always an effort. . . . And so it's almost like giving in to having a drink. (Tim)

> If I go to a party and there is alcohol available, I will drink it. I have a lot of friends who are very heavy drinkers, and they will always offer me a drink. And I never refuse, because I like drinking and I like the effects. (John)

Some respondents reported that they sometimes decreased their drinking if other people were using less alcohol than they themselves were accustomed to using: "I'd say that I tend to drink less when I'm around people who drink less and who I really like and really care about and have a well-developed social rapport with" (Gregory).

There were, of course, individuals whose drinking appeared to be unaffected by that of their peers. In the present study, these men were heavy, rather than light, drinkers. Not surprisingly, all of the currently abstinent recovering alcoholics said that "in the past," they had been solitary drinkers.

It was not uncommon for the men to report having used alcohol by themselves, at least occasionally. Almost half the men indicated that they sometimes drank alone. This does not mean, however, that they were all incipient alcoholics or that they divided their alcohol use equally between solitary drinking and social drinking. On the contrary, most of the men were basically social drinkers and only occasionally drank by themselves. When they did drink alone, it was often a way of relaxing or unwinding after coming home from work. For some men this was a daily ritual: "I come home and instantly make myself a drink, first thing," Jack said, in a description reminiscent of the opening scene from Doric Wilson's play, *A Perfect Relationship*, "and just sit down and it's just a form of unwinding. It's a must." For other respondents, having a drink immediately upon arriving home was a means of attempting to reduce job-related tensions. This was not a usual or consistent practice for most of them, and was often seen as a way of temporarily coping with an overwhelming situation. For example, Peter remarked, "Very occasionally at home when I'm uptight, I'll have a beer. That's probably once a month, something like that. . . . In other words, it isn't something that I just sort of do in the course of daily life." Paul told me that his home drinking had begun to accelerate as a result of the pressures of working with a new supervisor. When he realized what was happening to him, he sought psychiatric help in an attempt to find other ways of reducing anxiety.

Besides using alcohol to relax after a hard day, men who were primarily social drinkers sometimes drank when they were working around the house on weekends, when they were watching television, when eating solitary dinners, or when they were bored or frustrated.

Although anxiety, tension, and boredom encouraged increases in drinking, for the most part they were temporary or periodic causes of additional consumption, contributing little to the overall alcohol use of most respondents. Much more relevant to increases and decreases in individual drinking were changes in friendship networks, alterations in bar attendance, alcohol use on the part of one's companions, and the establishment or breakup of love relationships.

Responses to Heavy Drinking

Evidence from the interviews in this study, as well as from field observations, suggests that many gay men are reluctant to confront a problem drinker over his use of alcohol. For example, although 41% of the men in the study said that they had spoken to friends who seemed to have a drinking problem, they had done so only in isolated instances involving one friend, and they voiced their concerns so tactfully that the friend was able to ignore any advice on seeking help. The men were rarely forceful in confronting a companion with a drinking problem.

> TOM: Have you ever told friends you thought they had a drinking problem?
> SCOTT: My comments on the topic were pretty circumspect and diplomatic, I think.
> TOM: What kind of response did you get?
> SCOTT: Usually my comments were ignored.

When the men were asked why they had told friends they had a drinking problem, only four of them said their action was based on the amount their friends had drunk. This finding supports Warren's (1974) thesis that gay men do not consider heavy drinking to be problem drinking as long as it occurs within a social context. In fact, in order for the amount consumed to even be noticed by the men in this study, it had to be so extreme that the individual was unaware of his surroundings and could not function. Most commonly, others were only confronted if their behavior was extreme or its conse-quences were damaging (cf. Becker, 1963, pp. 12–13). Such in-stances included a series of arrests for drunken driving, jail senten-ces, the inability to control one's drinking, or violence:

> Somebody was drunk on their ass and started a fight with his lover in the bar. The bar was closing [and] he wouldn't leave . . . and he couldn't walk, so I took him up and threw him over my shoulder and carried him out. And put him in the car and drove him home. The next day he didn't remember a thing about it. . . . I sat him down and told him right in front of his lover, I said, "You are an alcoholic." He said, "No, I'm not." And I said, "You are. You go out every night and you get drunk and have blackouts and throw up, and you get belligerent. You don't remember what you do . . . and that's not right; you've got to get yourself some help." (Joe)

Fewer than a third of the men in the study reported having been told by others that they had a drinking problem, despite the fact that large numbers of them had worried about their own drinking. In fact, two men said regretfully, "I wish they would" (Ted) and "If they didn't, they should have" (Gregory). When respondents were told that they were drinking too much or that they had a drinking problem, it was most often done in a joking manner, rather than in a confrontational way.

> TOM: Have your friends ever told you that they thought you had a drinking problem?
> BEN: Not in a very serious manner. It was always . . . just kind of half joking, half being smart aleck, kind of goofing around. It was never very serious.

Problem drinkers typically take such criticism negatively, or ignore it altogether.

> TOM: How did you feel about what they were telling you, that you had a drinking problem?

CHUCK: I would say, "I know it, who doesn't these days?"

VINNIE: They were doing the same thing. It was hypocrisy.

Failure to confront problem drinkers is not confined to the gay world. Kraft (1981) found that 40% of his sample reported getting a buzz on or being tipsy or high two or more times a month and that 47% said that they had gotten drunk at least once during the previous month. Also, 36% of his students revealed at least one behavior problem related to drinking during the previous year. Yet only 3% of the respondents said they had been urged to get help during the year.

The central theme of this chapter is that other people influence one's drinking, at the very least by being part of the social context as it is perceived by the individual, whether gay or heterosexual.[5] Alcohol use is a social behavior for most people, whatever their sexual orientation, and their consumption tends to approximate that of their drinking group. There were, however, some differences between the gay men in this study and the heterosexuals studied by other researchers.

In contrast with studies of college students and others, drinking in bars took on greater importance for my respondents. The largest proportion of gays identified the bar as the context in which most of their drinking took place, and they were significantly more likely to be frequent bar visitors than heterosexuals were. For (presumably heterosexual) college students, most drinking occurred at parties. More than half of the gay respondents did say that drinking was expected at parties, but only 4% of them identified parties as their primary drinking situations. While consuming larger than usual amounts of alcohol at parties is common for heterosexuals, only a few gays did their heaviest drinking there. Drinking in their own homes (in social situations) and in those of friends was reported by a significant minority of men, but home drinking was less important than bar drinking. Like heterosexuals, the gay home drinkers were more likely to be heavy than light users of alcohol. Slightly more gays than heterosexuals reported solitary drinking as a usual practice. For both groups, confrontations with problem drinkers were generally avoided. The settings and situations in which alcohol use occurs will be examined in more specific detail in the following chapters.

4. <u>The Bar</u>

The Sultan's facade is unremarkable, blending in with the other stucco buildings in the "Pill Hill" section of Las Cumbres, so called because of the concentration of physicians' offices in the area. By about 10:00 on a weekend evening, the place begins to fill, as men drift in singly, and in couples and small groups. There are no lines of people awaiting admittance outside, as there sometimes are at several of the city's large, popular dance bars that attract young men in their twenties. The patrons of the Sultan are older business and professional men in their thirties, forties, and fifties. They are dressed casually and conservatively, in slacks and sport shirts. As someone enters, customers glance up, often exchanging a greeting with the newcomer as he makes his way to the bar. Most patrons seem to know one another; the Sultan has the atmosphere of a private club, drawing in regulars several nights a week.

The Sultan is a small establishment, and most nights it seems overcrowded. The kind of milling behavior common in the larger bars is absent, as is the overt cruising noticeable in other bars. The narrow rectangular room is dominated by a massive mahogany bar, running two-thirds of the length of the wall opposite the entrance. Halfway down the other long wall is a piano bar, the center of interest for the evening's entertainment. Three booths are squeezed in at the far end of the room, near a small alcove leading to a parking lot. Patrons stand in this tiny space that is further cramped by a cigarette machine, and spill out the rear door, blocking the movement of people attempting to use the restroom.

As the evening advances, the din of conversation increases. The air thickens with cologne, sweat, and body heat, and the cloud of cigarette smoke becomes overpowering. Annie, the regular piano player, sits down and begins to play, singing in a quavering voice. Men sitting around the piano bar join in, blending their baritones with her soprano. The songs are show tunes and others made popular by Barbra Streisand, Bette Midler, Frank Sinatra, and others. No rock and roll sung here.

After a few numbers, a man in his thirties, emboldened by alcohol and encouraged by his friends, gets up and moves around the bar to consult briefly with Annie. As she plays an introduction, he picks up a microphone and begins to sing "The Impossible Dream," from *The Man of La Mancha*, in a clear baritone. He takes his seat to enthusiastic applause and another patron takes his place. With time out for Annie's break, the singing goes on for another couple of hours. The crowd thins out by closing time, and another Saturday night at the Sultan is over.

Gay Bars in Paradise City

At any given time, Paradise City contains between thirty and forty gay bars. About three or four of these are primarily lesbian establishments, although some men do go to them. Her Place, for example, which has been operating for several years, is a favorite "home territory bar" (Cavan, 1966) for a number of older men who have lesbian friends.

Most gay bars in Paradise City are remarkably stable, some having lasted from the 1970s into the early 1990s, while others open and close very quickly. This phenomenon of quick bar shifts has been noted by a number of writers (Achilles, 1967; Cavan, 1966; Hooker, 1967). Cavan, for example, observes that sometimes the popularity of a given bar may change so abruptly that "one can find an establishment that was literally packed seven nights a week for some time to be virtually empty a month later, with many of its patrons at a new place that previously had little popularity" (p. 208). Achilles attributes these fluctuations in the fortunes of individual bars to fads, competition, police behavior and city politics, and the personalities and reputations of owners and bartenders. The political consciousness of the gay community also plays a role. For example, when the owner of a Del Parque bar was accused of discriminating against African Americans, the attendance at that bar and at another one he owns fell off sharply.

The number of gay bars in Paradise City is unusual. Most cities of comparable size have fewer than a dozen such establishments.

This large number of bars allows for a degree of specialization. There are, for example, dance bars such as the Pacific Coast and Gunsmoke; piano bars such as the Sultan and Numero Uno; country/western establishments like J. B.'s and Stomper's; and leather bars such as the Branding Iron, the Dungeon, and the Docks. Herald Square features drag shows, while the Drummer presents male go-go dancers. The Cabin remains open past 2:00 A.M. as an after-hours club for serving nonalcoholic beverages. Other bars are primarily places for cruising, while still others are relatively quiet "conversation" bars, "posing" bars, or neighborhood taverns. There are ethnic, class, and age variations among the bars as well. For example, the Brass Monkey attracts Hispanics, while Gunsmoke, which features an expensive laser light show, draws a wealthier, white, collegiate crowd. The Sultan, with its older, upper-middle-class clientele, is referred to as a "wrinkle" bar or "troll" bar by younger men.

Gay bars are found throughout Paradise City, but most of them are located either in the downtown area or in the adjacent Las Cumbres and Del Parque sections. These enclaves verify Hooker's (1967) observation that gays and the institutions that grow up to serve their needs are not randomly distributed, but that they tend to be clustered in certain areas. This clustering effect may be attributed, in part, to the bar-going habits of gay men, who tend to barhop (Hooker, 1967). Bar owners take advantage of this behavior by locating their businesses near each others'. The work of Levine (1979) on gay ghettos describes a similar pattern. Interestingly, some of the respondents in the present study told me that different groups of men tend to frequent different bar clusters and have little to do with one another, so that, for example, habitués of the downtown bars rarely visit the suburban establishments.

The Importance of the Bar

The social life of the men who participated in this study centered around interaction in the gay bar. The importance of bars in the lives of these men is reflected in the finding that all but two of them reported frequent visits. One of these men, who was in his late sixties, felt that he did not fit in because of his age. He occasionally went to bars but only with a friend. Such an excursion would normally be incorporated into an evening out, with dinner or a show. Even on these occasions, he would limit himself to one glass of wine and then leave early. The other man who no longer went to bars was a recovering alcoholic. He felt that if he did go, he would be strongly tempted to drink. The acknowledgment by the other recovering alcoholics that they still attended the bars even though they did not drink is clear evidence of the importance of these establishments in the gay community.[1]

When male homosexuals talk about the gay bar scene, they typically use the generic expression, "the bar." This term evokes emotions for gay people in a way that it does not for heterosexuals. It refers to a social institution around which people's very lives are organized and to which their daily schedules are oriented. Many men "live for the bar," as the focal point of their nonworking lives. In this sense, "the bar" is simultaneously a particular bar and a generic term, with implications reaching well beyond individual drinking establishments.

For gay men, especially those who are not in love relationships, the bar is a social center where friendship cliques meet to exchange gossip and information and to enjoy each other's company (Hooker, 1967), and is still the most common setting for this kind of interaction. In a Los Angeles study, for example, Fifield (1975) found that social activity revolved around the bars and that few bar patrons socialized in other settings. The problem, as Fifield sees it, is that the social options of gay people are severely limited. Read (1980) further notes the special importance of the homosexual tavern as a place where people can feel accepted. For Read, the essence of the bar is that it is "a setting in which it is possible to find and experience a commonality that contrasts with the world beyond the tavern's doors" (p. 69). That is, the attraction of the bar is not merely alcoholic or sexual; it is a place where a person can feel "normal." There, his homosexuality is accepted, taken as a given, and shared by others in the setting. It is the one place in which he does not have to worry about covering his feelings or being rejected for his sexuality. Thirty-nine percent of the men I interviewed mentioned a feeling of belonging as an important motivation for going to gay bars.

> Tom: What do you feel are your own needs that the bars help to fill?

TIM: One of them was . . . being a part of something. Definitely a
feeling of society, other people that I could relate to or get to
know.

PETER: In Paradise City, it's been . . . a feeling of belongingness,
sort of a community gathering place feeling and a community
that I really identify with and feel a part of.

The power of this function of the bar cannot be overemphasized.
As noted earlier, many gay people grow up with a sense of isolation;
they have feelings they cannot share with anyone, and they often
believe that they are the only ones in the world with homoerotic
attractions (Weinberg, 1983). Despite the fact that homophile organizations have existed for forty years in the United States (Yearwood &
Weinberg, 1979), a wider gay world has been formed only relatively
recently with institutions such as churches, restaurants, banks, and
the creation of gay holidays such as Gay Pride Week. More recently,
other organizations and alternatives have sprung up in reaction to
the AIDS epidemic. Yet for gays, the tavern has historically been
virtually the only place where group solidarity is expressed. The
gay bar has traditionally brought individuals together to deal as a
group with a common problem of adjustment: the normalization of
a stigmatized identity. It is, therefore, properly understood as the
focal point for the formation of a subculture (Cohen, 1955).

Achilles (1967) notes that the most important function of the bar
is the provision of a meeting place within which gays can comfortably
interact. "Without such a place to congregate," Achilles feels, "the
group would cease to be a group" (p. 230). The loss of the group,
either by its dissolution or by leaving it, may cause severe problems
for some gay men. Without such a group serving as an extended
family and providing emotional support, validation of one's nor-
malcy, and recreation, the individual would have a more difficult
time developing and maintaining gay identity (Nardi, 1982a). This
seems to be especially true for some gays who have very little to
do with heterosexuals except in work or school settings, and whose
associations are therefore limited to other gay people. Since the
bar is where they meet their friends and since they perceive few
alternatives for social interaction outside of the gay world, they are
effectively locked into the bar scene if they want any kind of a social
life at all. If they leave the bar, they may also abandon much of gay

life and become isolated from the gay world. This is apparent in the wistful remarks made by Bruce, who when asked if he had a group of gay friends, replied,

> I used to. I don't any longer. When I was hittin' the bars all the time, I had a group of gay friends, probably seven, eight, or nine people, that I saw on a regular basis. I don't have one of those friends today, because I quit going to gay bars. . . . Maybe if I start going back to the bars I will [have friends], but right now, no.

As Bruce indicates, people are bound to the bars through their friendship networks.

Bars are places to meet potential sexual partners and places to find entertainment. They may also fulfill more specialized functions such as loan office, restaurant, message reception center, and telephone exchange, and may facilitate the exchange of both legitimate and illegitimate goods and services (Achilles, 1967). In these functions, gay bars are no different from many heterosexual drinking establishments (Kingsdale, 1973; LeMasters, 1973; Prus, 1983; Roebuck & Spray, 1967). Prus (1983) writes that nongay "bars can be seen as small communities, with friendships and animosities, exchanges and barters, politicizing and gaming, recreation and work, intimacy and distancing, gossip and reputations, and deviance and control" (p. 462).

In a national Canadian household survey, Cosper et al. (1987) asked their respondents to choose the most important reason why they went to public drinking establishments. The largest proportion of frequent attenders (at least once a month) with a regular place to go said that they went to meet old friends (28.5%), followed by a smaller proportion who went for entertainment (24%), and the smallest group who went to accompany someone (15.1%). Other motivations for going to bars were eating (9.7%), relaxing (9.2%), drinking (5%), making new friends (4.8%), playing (2.3%), and passing the time (1.2%).

In the present study, gay men were asked, What do you feel are your own needs that the bars help to fill? Since no restrictions were placed on the number of replies per individual, some men identified several reasons for going to the bar. Thus, these responses are not exactly comparable to those of the Cosper et al. (1987) study. Of the total number of 132 responses, there were twenty-five mentions of going to the bars as "something to do," twenty-one mentions of the bar as a meeting place, twenty mentions of the bar as a setting in which to meet sexual partners, and eighteen mentions of the bar as a gathering place for the gay community. Other motives for attending the bars were to dance or listen to music (twelve mentions), to drink (eleven), to make new friends (ten), to have a good time (five), to combat loneliness (three), to relax and to express oneself (two mentions each), and to deal with pressure, to "escape," and to find excitement (one mention each). For both groups, then, social motivations and entertainment are the most important reasons for bar attendance, and drinking is not nearly as important. Gay men, however, see the opportunity to meet potential sexual partners and the ability to be with their own community as additionally important functions of the bar.

There are two important characteristics of gay bars that must be understood to appreciate how patrons' expectations and consequent interactions are structured. The first of these is that participation in the gay world is a leisure-time activity. Social interaction in the bar revolves around what Matza and Sykes (1961) call "subterranean values," those "which are in conflict with or in competition with other deeply held values but which are still recognized and accepted by many" (p. 716). While subterranean values such as the search for excitement and adventure are part of the larger American culture, they are segregated from more conventional values, and their expression is often compartmentalized (Matza & Sykes, 1961). Only among the very affluent, nonworking upper classes (the so-called jet set), juvenile delinquents, the gay world, and a few other subcultures do these values become a major focal concern (Miller, 1958) rather than remaining a minor underlying theme. Thus, the gay world must be understood as a play world, within which excitement and adventure are important gratifications. It is a self-indulgent scene in which the individual attempts to have his own physical, emotional, social, and recreational needs met.

The second characteristic of the bar is that as a leisure world, it is segregated from other aspects of an individual's life such as work and home, and, to some degree, from the larger majority community (Achilles, 1967). This separation occurs in two ways. First, bars are often located in out-of-the-way places such as waterfronts, less-traveled parts of the downtown area, or predominantly gay neighborhoods. In other cases, the bar protects its anonymity and that of its patrons by simply presenting an unremarkable appearance and thereby blending in with other establishments nearby (Achilles, 1967; Reitzes & Diver, 1982). Second, the bar scene is a late-night world. In Paradise City, few men arrive at the bar before 10:00 P.M., even though the bars close at 2:00 A.M., and some bar owners begin clearing the premises by about 1:45 A.M. Therefore, most of the intense social interaction and cruising occurs within the space of only a few hours. Thus, the bar is segregated, by time as well as by location, from other aspects of an individual's life. This separation allows a person to freely seek the gratification of his own needs within the clearly defined boundaries of the bar culture.

Entering the Bar Scene

Hooker (1967) has pointed out that gay bars "serve as induction and training and integration centers for the community" (p. 178). That is, men sometimes first publicly "come out" (i.e., acknowledge their homosexual orientation and develop a compatible self-identity) in a bar setting. Within the gay bar, individuals acquire "a body of knowledge which includes a set of common understandings—'what everybody knows [about being gay]'" (p. 178). The majority of men, however, do not usually come out in a bar context. Dank (1971), for example, found that 19% of the 180 men whom he surveyed reported having come out in a bar. However, since some men mentioned more than one setting, bars made up only about 10% of the total settings in which this had occurred. In another study of gay male identity, I found that few men had first come out in the bars (Weinberg, 1983). Instead, they clarified their self-identities by meeting gays in the neighborhood, in gay community centers, and in gay student organizations, and by discussing their feelings with others, heterosexuals as well as homosexuals. Only after having decided that they were, in fact, gay, did they begin to frequent the bars. In the present study, the median age of coming out was nineteen (with a range of eleven to forty-two years), while the median age of first attending gay bars regularly was twenty-one (with a range of fifteen to sixty-five years). Although a few men felt that the bars had facilitated their self-acceptance, most of them had come out in other contexts, such as the military, at work, in high school or college, with childhood friends, or by meeting homosexuals in a wide variety of other settings. After coming out, however, the bar serves as an important setting for learning about the gay world. A number of men in the present study addressed this issue:

> The bar scene eased my way further out. It gave me more social contacts than I was able to have before. (Bruce)

> Seeing other gay people and identifying with some of their behavior, mannerisms, personalities, reminded me somewhat of myself, some of my sensitivities or my awarenesses. I think that contributed to my awareness of myself, who I really was, and sort of forced me to deal with myself. (Robert)

The men learned about gay bars in a number of different ways. Most commonly, they were taken there by homosexual friends. Others found out about the existence or whereabouts of gay bars from former sexual partners, from other gay people, or even from heterosexuals.

While some men had few problems associated with their initial visits to the bars, others frequently reported having been nervous and fearful. Generally, they were afraid of the unknown and anxious about possible discovery:

> I know when I first came out and first started going to the bars, and I'd go to the bars with various different guys, I was scared shitless of going to one by myself. You know, I was still new to it, and I didn't really know what to expect. I didn't know if everybody was going to stare at me or if everybody'd jump on me or what— fear of the unknown. (Frank)

Early visits to gay bars are, therefore, often sporadic and surreptitious.

> Том: When you first started going to the bar, were you going in any consistent way?
>
> Ben: No. It was pretty [much] when I got up the guts to do it. The nerve to go there. The nerve to park a couple blocks away so that no one could see my car parked out front or parked anywhere. I would be very clandestine about the whole thing. You know, walking in very quickly, going to the part of the bar that was not very well lit, and trying to pretty much keep a low profile.

Ben's behavior when he first began going to the bars illustrates some of the techniques described by Lofland (1972) in her discussion of self-management in public settings. These techniques are utilized by "the lone individual who must . . . make his way in a location with which he is generally unfamiliar among others whom he does not know" (p. 94) in order to "minimize the dangers of 'stranger-filled public settings'" (p. 98). "The individual," she writes, "enters and moves rapidly into the setting without a pause. . . . The entire body, head included, is fully directed into the setting, as though the individual were following a tunnel running right through the middle of the setting" (p. 102). By so doing, the person "prevents himself from taking much notice of those around him and avoids any full realization of the number of strangers who are looking at him" (p. 105).

As a man learns some of the primary norms and expectations of the bar scene, he gradually gets over his nervousness and learns to relax. He meets other people, makes acquaintances, develops friendships, and often experiences positive feedback on his social presentation of self, making the bar an attractive place to be. Being admired is an important inducement to bar attendance, especially when men first begin going to them:

> When I came out in the first bar, it was essentially the kind of admiration that I got from these older guys [that made bars appealing]. Admiration and validation and that kind of stuff. And it was social, too. That was the beginning. Then when I got comfortable with at least trying out cruising with people my own age or less, what drew me to those bars was the fact that they were crowded, the fact that there were just a lot of really attractive guys and just a sense of this incredible number of possible people to go home with. (Peter)

Over time, the individual becomes increasingly sophisticated as he learns to handle himself in bar situations. He becomes self-confident, sometimes bolder and less often shy within the all-gay setting. At this point, bar visitation usually stabilizes. Although a few men said that their bar going had increased or remained the same over time, most of them reported that they were currently going out less frequently than they had in the past. They accounted for this change in a number of ways. Some men said that they had become "burned out" on the bars. This usually means one of two things: either the bar has become so familiar that it is no longer a novelty and is therefore boring, or the individual is no longer the "new man in town," so that the attention he may have received when he first began going to the bar is no longer forthcoming. Other men said that changing jobs, developing friendships outside the bar, moving farther away from the primary bar areas, or lacking money have contributed to a decrease in bar attendance. Several men said that they were currently in a love relationship and that they simply had little time for bars.

Interaction in the Bar

When the men in this study first entered the gay bar world, they had already been drinking for a few years. Alcohol use also preceded coming out for many respondents. The median age for first drinking in a frequent way (i.e., at least once a week) for these men was eighteen, with a range of twelve to sixty years. The men had learned to use alcohol in a variety of contexts, the most important of which were with high school or college friends, with family, or in the military. Other men identified situations, such as being under stress or away from home, rather than specific social contexts or occasions, as having contributed to their initial use of alcohol. One respondent noted that although he had been drinking since the age of eighteen as a college student, his "real" drinking began during business lunches. Interestingly, only six men identified the gay bar as the setting within which they first began to drink.

Even though few men began drinking in the bars, these settings did affect alcohol consumption, at least in terms of learning new drinking styles and coming to attach new meanings to alcohol use and alcohol-related behavior. For example, one of the things a man first learns when he enters the bar scene is that the kind of alcoholic drink he buys must fit the image that is cultivated by the particular establishment and its patrons. He learns that imaging practices (Kamel, 1983) are extremely important in developing an acceptable presentation of self in the bar. Delph (1978), for instance, describes some of the ways alcohol is used as a prop to enhance one's image within the bar setting. Thus, by holding a beer bottle "with a full hand rather than by a few fingers" (p. 119) bar patrons contribute to the consistency of the masculine image they are attempting to project. One man noted that in a masculine-oriented leather/levi bar he would never drink anything "that comes in a stem or glass." To do so would be to violate the implicitly shared understandings about what is appropriate (i.e., "masculine") behavior in that setting. Most of the time, of course, men are not explicitly told what is correct and expected behavior in a given setting. They must do interpretative work to make sense of what is going on. They observe others and look for clues; in a sense, they socialize themselves.

A number of men indicated that they often felt a subtle pressure to drink alcoholic beverages, an observation also made by Warren (1974).[2] Some of them voiced a good deal of ambivalence over this. For example, Ted told me:

> If I go to a bar, it's nearly impossible not to drink. Well, I have gone to bars and haven't drunk, but also, it's a situation around you. . . . I've gone in just to drink water and stuff,[3] but I don't have as good a time, because everyone is drunk and I think I have to be. It's a matter of—I don't think it's conforming with them, but I think it's a situation of the setting, too.

I experienced the kinds of peer pressure described by Ted several times. Attempts to get me to drink were most often made by friends who were heavy drinkers, rather than by those who were moderate users. There were occasions when, despite my better judgment, I gave in to repeated offers of a drink rather than continue to resist them:

> One night, Sully, P. J., Hal, Phil, and I decided to go out dancing. We started at the Brass Monkey, a long-established, popular bar located in Las Cumbres. I ordered my usual tonic with a twist of lime, and stood around watching the dancers and talking with Sully. After awhile, P. J. came back from the dance floor. "What are you drinking?" he asked. I told him. "You shouldn't be drinking that stuff," he said. "Let me buy you a real drink." I responded that I was fine, and that I was concerned about getting home safely, since I was not a drinker. "Don't worry about it," he said. "One won't hurt you." He came back twice more over the next half hour. I finally gave in and he bought me a beer.

The amorphous kinds of pressures mentioned by gay men actually derive from a number of different sources: the importance of impres-

sion management, discussed above, the use of alcohol to facilitate
cruising, the expectations of friendship groups, and a variety of
inducements provided by bar management.

Alcohol Use, Cruising, and Sexual Risk

In addition to its social function, the gay bar has traditionally
served as what Hooker (1967) calls a free market. She uses this
concept as a metaphor for the exchange of sexual services negotiated
within the bar setting. The "essential feature" of these transactions
is "the standardized expectation that sex can be had without obligation or commitment" (p. 176). This does not, however, occur in a
random or haphazard fashion. Rather, Achilles (1967) notes that the
bar serves to facilitate as well as to regulate the formation of sexual
relationships, which it does in a way that is safer and more respect-
able than making contacts in parks, streets, and public restrooms.
"The individual may feel much less anxiety and guilt," according to
Achilles, "if he is able to carry on this aspect of his life in an organized
framework of social norms and values. The bar is the homosexual
equivalent of the USO or youth club, where the rating and dating
process may unfold in a controlled and acceptable manner" (pp.
231–232). Achilles' point is illustrated by Peter, a professional man,
who comments on the way some contacts are made at the Sultan,
the middle-class piano bar that was described earlier:

> At the Sultan I've met some people, but we do stuff like instead of
> giving our first names and saying, "Hope to see you again," we
> exchange cards. . . . And people say stuff like, "I would really like
> to get to know you better," and when people say that at the Cabin
> they mean, "Your place or mine?" typically. People have said that
> at the Sultan, and it's, "When are you free for lunch? Oh, damn! I
> don't have my calendar." So it's not primarily cruising in the sense
> of sex that night but more in the sense of really meeting people,
> and a relationship or whatever will develop from that.

Contacts such as those described above are sometimes initiated
at the Sultan by buying someone a drink, often mediated by a
bartender:[4]

Phil, Sully, and I had gone out barhopping and stopped at the Sultan. Phil seemed to know everyone there and went from patron to patron, flirting with some men and sitting on the laps of others. Later, he was persuaded to get up and sing, which he did to enthusiastic applause. Toward the end of the evening, the bartender presented him with a drink, indicating that it came from one of two men in their sixties sitting at the end of the piano bar. Phil took the drink without acknowledging the source. About half an hour later, he went over to the men and chatted briefly and politely with them, indicating by his physical distance from them, the uncharacteristic lack of animation in his facial expressions, and the time that had elapsed since the receipt of the drink that he was not interested in them. We left a few minutes later.

In bars that serve a younger and less affluent crowd than the Sultan, sexual contacts tend to be more aggressive and impersonal. In large establishments such as dance bars, where the noise level precludes conversation, men are continually moving about in search of sexual partners. The physical design of the bar and the arrangement, or lack, of furniture facilitate the flow of traffic and enable patrons to make contacts with each other (Delph, 1978). Milling is often consciously encouraged by the bar's management, since it tends to increase alcohol consumption as part of a rhythm of partner-seeking behavior. Richard describes how his alcohol consumption is integrated into his cruising behavior.

> Tom: Can you describe a typical night at the bars? What would it be like? What would you be doing? What would you be drinking?
>
> Richard: It would be probably, I'd leave the house about 9:30 and arrive at the Pacific Coast about 10:00, 10:05. I would stand at the top for a minute and just look at the crowd for about, oh, five, six minutes, getting comfortable; and then I finally would walk to the back of the bar—they have a back bar—and order a tall gin and tonic. And then I would proceed to come to the front of the bar and kind of stand in this particular area that I usually like to stand in. And I'd have one and just kind of look around at the crowd. And then I'd definitely get a second drink and continue the same behavior. And then the third drink. By the time I'm on the third drink, I'm definitely cruising pretty heavy, actually walking around. And usually when I get to the fourth, I ask someone to dance. Or if I see someone I know, we might chitchat, "How you been? What's going on?" Just

> general conversation like that. And usually by the fourth drink
> I've asked someone to dance and we're dancing. I'm deciding
> whether or not to keep the interest or find someone else. He's
> doing the same thing. And if I'm going to go home with the
> person, I usually try to do it by 1:30, 2:00. . . . That's usually
> a typical night.

Like Richard, almost all participants establish standard procedures for preparing to go out, develop regular routes that include
favorite bars, and build up routine patterns of behavior within the
bars. These behaviors include habituated methods of obtaining
drinks, milling about, styles of greeting acquaintances, and standing
or sitting in favorite turf-like locations. Richard's behavior includes
"taking a reading" and "reaching a position," which are common
features of self-management in public described by Lofland (1972).
However, the length of time he takes to do this, according to Lofland,
is atypical since "Americans seem to feel constrained to take readings
as quickly as possible and to do so in such a way as to suggest that
they are not doing so" (p. 101). The "frank, unabashed assessments,"
such as those described by Richard, "are rarely observed" (p. 102).

The role of alcohol in disinhibition has been noted by a number
of writers (Molgaard, Nakamura, Hovell, & Elder, 1988; Reinarman
& Leigh, 1987; Stall, McKusick, Wiley, Coates, & Ostrow, 1986).
Some of my respondents reported that if they were looking for a
sexual partner, they tended to drink more than they would ordinarily. They said that alcohol helped them relax and relieved their
anxieties over possible rejection. This relatively small number of
men who used alcohol to facilitate cruising saw drinking as a way
to reduce their anxieties about making sexual contacts.

> TOM: How would your going, say to cruise, affect how much you
> drink and what you drink?

> PAUL: It affects me. I have to drink a little more. I have to drink
> two beers. Sometimes even three, to be able to really cruise.
> To be able to really lose my inhibitions about what I'm doing.

> GREGORY: Yeah, I think there's a definite difference. I tend to drink
> more if I'm going to pick someone up, I think, because I think
> that has to do with my own hangups about doing that. You
> know, about just going up to somebody and saying, "Do you

want to go home?" I think I'm not real comfortable with that, and I think I tend to drink more, you know, to be a little more pliant.

Reducing anxiety in order to make sexual contacts does not, however, seem to be an important motivation for drinking for most men. First, a similar number of men said that they would reduce their use of alcohol in a cruising situation because excessive alcohol consumption would make them less attractive, impotent, and because "it's difficult to trick when you can't walk out the door" (Erik). Second, although most men indicated that they were usually open to making sexual contacts, they did not go to bars primarily for sex. Fewer than half the men reported that the bars served this function for them. Using gay bars as a sexual marketplace appears to be most important for those men who are just beginning to frequent them, and it is thus intimately intertwined with a more general socialization into the wider gay world. Most men stated that they made sexual contacts in other settings:

> When I was younger, I cruised the gay bars, not only to see my friends, but to find sex. I don't do that any longer. I don't have to go to a gay bar to find sex. I know how to find it when I want it, where I want it, and with whom I want it. And so, therefore, I don't need to go to a gay bar to pick up someone anymore. If I do, well, fine. If I don't, well, it's immaterial. So, yeah, it's changed. (Bruce)

In an era when cruising can have fatal consequences, the link between alcohol use and sexual risk taking is a very real concern (Nardi, 1991). Molgaard et al. (1988), for instance, point out that alcohol abuse is an important potential risk factor in HIV infection. Noting that the rate of alcoholism in the gay community may exceed 30%, they state that since it exerts "deleterious effects upon immune regulation, heavy alcohol consumption may decisively mitigate the susceptibility and resistance to HIV infection and overt expression of AIDS. Assuming a high rate of alcoholism among homosexuals and the immunoincompetence conferred by excessive drinking, alcohol addiction may be placing individuals at high risk for acquired immunodeficiency" (p. 1147). Additionally, alcohol may cloud a man's judgment, so that he might take chances under its influence that he otherwise would not. Molgaard et al. (1988) believe that "alcohol use may represent a risk for AIDS and other sexually transmitted diseases (STDs) because of its likely effects on sexual behavior" (p. 1149). A number of recent studies support this speculation. Most of this research, however, utilizes correlational methods, and a causal relationship has not been definitively established.

While many gay and bisexual men appear to have modified their high-risk sexual behaviors, at least in the larger cities (Connell & Kippax, 1990; Martin, 1987; McKusick, Horstman, & Coates, 1985; Siegel, Mesagno, Chen, & Christ, 1989; Stall, Coates, & Hoff, 1988), there are still a number of factors and subpopulations linked with high risk taking. In a panel study of several populations of gay men in San Francisco from 1984 to 1985, Stall et al. (1986) found a highly significant relationship between drinking and high-risk sexual behavior. Men who were at high risk were almost two and a half times more likely to use alcohol during sexual activity than those who were at no risk. However, the researchers were unable to conclusively prove causation.

In a more recent study, Stall, Heurtin-Roberts, McKusick, Hoff, and Lang (1990) discovered that heterosexual male and female bar habitués as well as homosexual male bar patrons have a high risk of HIV transmission compared to other samples of sexually active heterosexuals and gay men. As in earlier research on gay male samples (Stall et al. 1986), the highest risk for HIV infection was incurred by both heterosexuals and homosexuals who engaged in sexual activity under the influence of drugs and alcohol.

In a questionnaire study conducted in gay bars in three small southern cities, Kelly, St. Lawrence, Brasfield, Stevenson, et al. (1990) found a high rate of sexual risk taking despite a high degree of factual knowledge about HIV transmission among those answering their questions. Reported rates of risk taking were two to three times higher than those found in the larger cities. Similar results have been reported in other studies conducted in smaller cities. For example, Ruefli, Yu, and Barton (1992b) found high levels of sexual risk taking among a sample of 487 gay men in Buffalo, New York, compared to lower levels among other samples in the large AIDS epicenters of New York City, Los Angeles, and San Francisco.[5] Ruefli et al. (1992b) linked risk taking to drinking. Compared to men who took no sexual risks, "high risk takers were more likely to be frequent bargoers, heavier drinkers, and use drugs more frequently" (p. 101). Yet it was not alcohol use itself that was important.

Rather, "sexual risk taking was . . . associated with the percentage of drinking done in bars" (Ruefli, Yu, & Barton, 1992a, p. 1). Thus, it was the drinking context that seemed to be the critical variable, because the bar is still the most important setting in which gay men search for sexual partners. It is also the setting in which men are most likely to have sex with someone they have just met. According to Ruefli et al. (1992a), the bars "attract men who tend to have higher levels of sexual opportunisity and sexual risk taking" (p. 9). Sexual opportunisity is defined as "the likelihood that an individual would search for and take advantage of, opportunities for sexual risk taking" (p. 5), while risk taking refers to sexual activities that carry the possibility of HIV transmission, such as unprotected anal sex.

I did not ask the men I interviewed about specific high-risk sexual acts they may have performed while under the influence of alcohol, or how they felt alcohol affected the type of sex in which they were likely to engage. Yet in a spontaneously offered statement, one of them illustrated the attraction of the bars as a setting both for sexual opportunisity and risk taking:

> Sometimes there is an aversion to talking about the tremendous association of sexual adventures . . . with drinking. . . . It was in the bars that I found what I wanted, and it was through the drinking that I could get uninhibited enough to make whatever proposals I was going to make, or to receive whatever proposals were made to me with some degree of maybe getting through all the fear, and whatever else, in getting home together. . . . I like the warm naughty atmosphere of the bars. I like the . . . threats and the danger. (Joel)

Some research has not demonstrated a relationship between alcohol use and sexual risk taking. Using discriminant analysis in a longitudinal study of asymptomatic gay men in New York City, Siegel et al. (1989) found that "the most important predictor of persistent risky behavior" was drug use during sex (p. 566). Alcohol use only approached significance. However, in contrast to their questions about drug use, the researchers did not directly ask about drinking within sexual contexts. Had they done so, "patterns of abuse that encourage sustained risky behavior (e.g., repeated intoxication) may have emerged with more refined measurement of alcohol and poly-substance abuse" (p. 566). Similarly, Leigh (1990) found that risky sex among gay men was related to the proportion of sexual activity involving cocaine and other drugs; a similar relationship did not appear between alcohol use and risky sex.

What, then, is the relationship between alcohol use and sexual risk taking? Some studies have found a correlation between the two, or at least between drinking contexts and risk taking for both gays and heterosexuals. In the extreme, chronic alcohol abuse has been linked in a few case studies with conscious attempts to commit suicide through contracting AIDS (Flavin, Franklin, & Frances, 1986; Frances, Wikstrom, & Alcena, 1985). Yet researchers have failed, so far, to establish a causal connection between these variables. Some writers have speculated that drinking and high-risk sex may be interconnected in complex ways, as, for example, through a variety of intervening or antecedent variables. All of the investigators I have cited acknowledge problems in their research, most commonly difficulties in assuring the representativeness of their samples. My own view is that there is enough consistency in the findings across these studies to assume that high-risk sexual behavior and drinking are related in some way, and if drinking does not directly cause risk taking, it at least accompanies and exacerbates this behavior.

Contracting AIDS is a real possibility in Paradise City, as it is everywhere today. In 1981, only two deaths from AIDS were reported in Paradise County. A year later, the deaths had doubled, and from then on, the increase was exponential. By the mid-1980s, there were over 200 deaths, and by 1988, the annual death toll had risen to over 400. By the end of the decade, there had been a drop in deaths, and the figure for 1990 was less than 250. While bar attendance had dropped during the latter half of the 1980s, the bars were once again filled by the early 1990s. The impression of my friends in Paradise City is that a higher number of bar patrons than ever before are now drinking fruit juices and mineral water instead of alcohol. It will be interesting to see how this trend will affect cruising, still an important activity in the bars, as well as high-risk behavior.

Backroom Bars

One difference between the drinking establishments in Paradise City and those in larger metropolitan areas such as New York City and San Francisco lies in the function of the backroom bars.

In the past, bars in those cities that specialized in the sadomasochistic "leathersex" scene had back bars where high-risk sexual behavior of all kinds occurred. These settings appear to have lost their popularity (Israelstam & Lambert, 1984) since the mid-1980s, however, in light of an increasing concern about AIDS. In Paradise City, the back bar is simply another venue for drinking.

Friends, the Bar, and Drinking

The linkages between the bar, the group, and the individual have been noted. The bar provides a setting within which groups form and are maintained, and the group serves the individual as a source of emotional and social support, while validating sexual identity. In this context, friends strongly influence drinking behavior because, as Nardi (1982a) has pointed out, the group's expectations and attitudes in general are important. Friends influence bar visitation and migration patterns; barhopping and settling in a single bar tend to be strongly affected by the wishes of one's close companions. A third of the men, for instance, said that they usually visited more than one bar only if their friends wanted to barhop or if they did not find any friends in the first bar they entered. The settings in which the men made friends were linked to the frequency as well as to the amount of alcohol use. The men who had met friends in bars drank more frequently and consumed more drinks at a time than did the respondents who had not made friends in bars (see tables 2 and 3).

Friends influence each other's drinking in a number of ways: the amount of time they spend in bar settings, the importance they place on alcohol as a sign of sociability, and the ways they use alcohol to show acceptance and approval of each other. For example, some men said that the practice of buying friends drinks put them under pressure to consume alcohol and made them feel obligated to reciprocate. Many of them said that this practice kept them in the bar longer than they would have ordinarily stayed. As Hal put it, "You turn around and there's another drink there. Maybe you were getting ready to leave, you know, so you stay and talk a little longer. That type of thing." To refuse a proffered drink is bad form, as is failure to return the gesture.

Some men feel coerced, albeit subtly, by this situation. A part

Table 2.   Frequency of Drinking by Setting in Which Friends
Are Made

Frequency of Drinking	Friends Made in Bar Settings		Friends Made in Nonbar Settings Only	
	n^{a}	%	n	%
2 times a week or less	2	9	10	55
3 to 6 times a week	9	41	5	28
Every day	11	50	3	17
TOTAL	22	100	18	100

Note: Chi-square test of independence with 2 df = 10.76 ($p<.01$).
[a]Six self-identified recovering alcoholics, who were evenly divided in terms of where they made friends, have been excluded from this analysis because they were abstinent at the time of the study.

Table 3.   Number of Drinks When Drinking by Setting in
Which Friends Are Made

Number of Drinks	Friends Made in Bar Settings		Friends Made in Nonbar Settings Only	
	n^{a}	%	n	%
1 to 3 drinks	8	36	16	89
4 drinks or more	14	64	2	11
TOTAL	22	100	18	100

Note: Chi-square test of independence with 1 df = 11.38 ($p<.01$).
[a]Six self-identified recovering alcoholics, who were evenly divided in terms of where they made friends, have been excluded from this analysis because they were abstinent at the time of the study.

of this pressure is the feeling the men sometimes expressed of being left out of the interaction and unable to communicate well with others if their friends are using alcohol and they are not. This feeling provides a strong impetus to drink. Thus, men are linked to the bar, and consequently to drinking, through their friendship networks.

Buying rounds and encouraging others to drink is not, of course, confined to gay bars (Prus, 1983). Yet there may be some differences between gays and heterosexuals in the relationship between buying rounds and felt pressure to drink. In an ethnographic study of young adults' drinking groups in Glasgow, Scotland, Aitken (1985) noted that only 6% of his sample were members of groups in which overt pressures to consume or buy drinks were observed. This was the case even though most drinkers were members of groups in which round buying was common. Those pub attenders who said that they sometimes drank more than they intended (57% of males and 29% of females) had difficulty in explaining why they overindulged. "However, those who attempted to [explain] rarely mentioned pressures from others or round-buying procedures" (Aitken, 1985, p. 453). Among those groups in which overt pressures were observed, however, there was a tendency for individuals to consume more alcohol.

Bar Inducements

Opening a gay bar is a calculated risk. Bars can be lucrative ventures, depending on the right combination of location and personnel, but they are likely to be very short-lived. Thus, bar owners and management attempt to maximize their profits while they can by offering a variety of inducements to encourage attendance and drinking. Among these are dance floors and music, pinball machines, electronic games and pool tables, special prices on drinks, "kegger" parties,[6] "theme" nights,[7] and free or nominally priced meals. Some of the men mention these inducements as important reasons for patronizing one bar rather than another. They even organize their weekly activities around the sorts of entertainment provided by the bar. For example, the Dungeon served Sunday chicken dinners for a price of fifty cents. Daniel stated that he planned his bar visits and drinking to take advantage of this meal. He explained how his weekly schedule was oriented to bar inducements:

> On any given night I go out, there is a free kegger. [There is one] at a bar on Tuesday nights, so I go there and have three beers. I'll go out on Friday or Saturday night and have three beers. And then on Sunday, when they have a real cheap chicken dinner, I go. There's a big crowd there, so I go there and have three beers, about three beers.

While the sorts of inducements mentioned above are obviously important in attracting business, the men in the present study put greater emphasis on the clientele who frequent the bar, the atmosphere found there (which is also partially defined by the patrons, as well as by such things as an indefinable ambience, a feeling of congeniality and being comfortable there), and the attitudes of bar owners and bartenders. Of a total of 139 responses to the question, What makes a particular bar appealing to you? (some men identified several criteria as being important to them), there were thirty-six mentions of the type of clientele, twenty-six mentions of music and dancing, twenty-two mentions of the bar atmosphere, and nineteen mentions of the attitudes of bar owners and bartenders. Other criteria used by the men included the bar's decor or physical design (twelve mentions), the presence of pool tables, video games and pinball machines (four), a large number or diversity of patrons (four), uncrowded conditions (three), whether or not they felt comfortable there (three), the type and quality of drinks (two), the availability of intelligent conversation (two), the presence of male go-go dancers (two), the bar's cleanliness (two), the bar's reputation (one), and whether it was possible to be left alone while drinking (one).

From what these men say, the major task of the successful bar owner is figuring out what type of clientele would attract potential customers, and then creating the proper atmosphere to attract that kind of clientele (Achilles, 1967; Hooker, 1967).[8] This is managed to some extent by the location of the bar, but also depends on the staff the bar owners hire. The bar's reputation and the social types it attracts (e.g., leathermen, older affluent professionals, younger men, etc.) are strongly influenced by the personalities, reputations, and social characteristics of its personnel.

Bartenders

A large number of men in the study said that the attitudes of bartenders were important considerations in choosing a bar. They included such things as the friendliness of the bartenders, their ability to remember one's name and preferred drinks, and their general pleasantness as significant factors.

> TOM: What makes a particular bar appealing to you?
> HAL: The type of clientele that goes there and the bartender.

TOM: What is there about the bartenders that you find appealing?

HAL: Ah, I think it's friendliness. It depends on the type. Some bartenders don't give a damn; others treat you like a friend. And I think that makes a difference when you're out.

TOM: Do these people get to know you and get to know your preference?

HAL: Right. Yeah, they take time to find something out about you.

The bars to which Hal goes tend to fit into Cavan's (1966) category of home territory bars, which "are used as though they were the private retreat for some special group" (p. 205). In these places the bartender would appear to be more crucial to attracting a following than in the much larger and more anonymous disco bars. In the specific bars mentioned by Hal, Her Place and the Sultan, the bartenders (and in the case of the Sultan, the barmaids and the regular piano player as well) know many of the patrons by name and are familiar with their likes and dislikes and their favorite drinks.

I experienced the professional friendliness of the bar staff, so important to Hal, when he and P. J. took me to the Sultan for the first time and introduced me to William, the bartender:

> William began chatting with me in a very friendly way. He asked where I was from, and we discovered that we hailed from the same eastern state. After several minutes of conversation, he moved on to some other customers. About ten minutes later, I was startled to hear over the loud-speaker: "Let's all welcome Tom from Eastern City, who's here tonight for the first time." During the course of the evening, he periodically checked my drink, always remembering to address me by my first name.

Some men find this attentiveness flattering and conducive to an increase in drinking. It is one of a number of ways in which bartenders attempt to encourage the customer to spend his money on alcoholic beverages. Another technique, noted by Delph (1978), is to provide lower prices or "drinks on the house" to desirable patrons, which not only encourages drinking, but attracts a particular clientele as well. In addition, a number of respondents noted that they attended specific bars because certain bartenders made extra-strong drinks, especially for them. As Prus (1983) points out, "Regular patrons (and especially those defined as privileged through management or staff contacts) expect to receive preferential treatment over strangers and occasional patrons" (p. 462). One of the techniques used by bartenders in some of the smaller neighborhood bars to increase alcohol consumption is to encourage the idea that the bar is "home" and that the people there are participating in a small private party:

> Bob told me about a new bar that had just opened up close by, on the outskirts of one of the beach communities, and suggested that we go there and say hello to Jim. Bob said that this had become his new "neighborhood bar."
>
> When we got there in the early afternoon, the bar was empty except for Jim, two or three other patrons, and the bartender. Jim was already quite intoxicated, as was another man and the bartender. They had apparently been drinking since late morning, and were joking and laughing.
>
> Jim came around the bar and began to play bartender, serving drinks to the other men. The bartender then played customer. After awhile he began to ask, and later demand, that everyone buy him wine "shooters," shot glasses of the beverage, which he quickly downed.

The kind of play and role switching observed above is not unique to gay settings. Prus (1983), in his ethnographic study of bars, notes that

> not only may there be some interchanging of roles over the course of an evening (e.g., a patron leaves a group of drinking companions to assume his duties as a waiter or an entertainer becomes a patron between shows), but people occupying the roles of patron, staff and entertainer at any particular time may influence the drinking activities of people occupying the other roles. (p. 462)

At least as important as a bartender's friendliness is his physical attractiveness, which draws and often holds certain types of customers, especially older men. Their flirting and hints of potential sexual favors often seduce drinkers into staying at the bar much longer than they otherwise would. For example, Joel said that he used to frequent one particular bar "because I was in love with the bartender."

Bartenders themselves are aware of the belief that they are sexually available:

Don, an attractive young man in his early twenties, had recently joined our support group. He had been brought into the group by Hal, a member in his forties, who had a crush on him. Don and I were standing around after a meeting and making small talk. He mentioned that he was a bartender in a popular bar and began to talk about some of the problems of his profession. "You know what they say about bartenders," he said. I looked at him, puzzled. Realizing my confusion, he said, "Everybody thinks that we're promiscuous." He went on to explain to me that some of his customers came on to him at the bar, expecting him to go home with them after closing time, and that this had become a real annoyance.

The bartender and social control.   The role of the bartender is not limited to serving and encouraging the consumption of alcoholic beverages. One of his most important functions is as an agent of social control, defusing disputes (Cavan, 1966) and ensuring that behavior in the bar stays within acceptable bounds. Like a police officer, he is concerned with maintaining a "clean beat." An important reason for this is that gay bars are still subject to harassment and raids by official representatives of the larger community. For example, police frequently ticket cars parked outside gay bars, both in Paradise City and elsewhere, and respondents have reported being pulled over only a few blocks from the bar and even having been arrested for "drunk parking" (i.e., they were intoxicated but had not started their cars) in front of gay establishments.

Bartenders in gay bars, therefore, are careful not to give the police any pretext to look for violations. They learn to use a variety of techniques to anticipate and deal with potential trouble. Patrons who drink to excess are handled in a number of different ways, according to how well they are known by the bartenders. A number of men, for instance, said that some bartenders who know them will call a taxi or make other arrangements for them to get home safely. Another way of controlling heavy drinking that is utilized by bar staff who are well acquainted with the individual is to tease him about drinking too much, or to provide gentle hints that it is time to go:

> I have had a couple of bartender friends who are very close friends, and they tease me. . . . I wouldn't really say they're cutting me off, but usually I drink some coffee before I leave the bar, and every now and then they'll just automatically bring me a cup of coffee.

Gay Men, Drinking, and Alcoholism

> You know, I don't think it's because I've had too much to drink; it's more or less just because it's time for me to go home. You know, they just assume I'm going home at that time, or close to that time. (Hal)

When the bartender does not know the individual well, or if he is known to be troublesome—or if he possesses undesirable social characteristics such as being older, unattractive, or is unaccompanied by friends—his removal from the bar may be swift and more direct. In this case, the need to keep a clean beat may supercede any concerns for the individual's feelings or safety:

> One Wednesday night at about 10:30, Lee and I were in J. B.'s, a denim bar on the edge of the downtown area. We were killing time by playing pinball and drinking drafts. The bar to our right, which ran almost the length of the room, was completely occupied, so that there must have been at least twenty people present. At the back of the room, where the bar ended, there was a pool table. A tall, muscular man in his mid-twenties, obviously a body builder, was playing pool with a woman clad in denim.
> Suddenly, we heard a loud thud. We looked up and focused on the end of the bar near the back door. Instantly, the bartender flew around the bar, grabbed a fallen patron by a leg, and unceremoniously dragged him through the curtain shrouding the back door and out into the parking lot. All of this was accomplished in a matter of no more than ten seconds.
> The bar patrons glanced up momentarily and then resumed their conversations.

The bartender is a pivotal figure, whose personal characteristics have much to do with the success of a gay bar. The ways he handles clientele and controls the interaction in the bar, from providing drinks to facilitating introductions to dealing with potentially troublesome incidents, all serve to win him a following of customers (Achilles, 1967), without which the bar's chances of survival would be slim.

Leaving the Bar Scene

While few men ever withdraw completely from the world of the gay bar, many of them do reduce the frequency of their visits and curtail the amount of time spent in these places. As I have previously noted, the demands of employment, financial problems, a change of residence, new friendships, and involvements in love relationships may all contribute to a decrease in bar attendance. The most important of these factors, however, are the same ones that influence bar attendance in the first place: one's relationships with other people. Gay men go to bars primarily for social reasons, and the cliques that form around particular establishments perform important functions for the individual. As Gregory told me, "There was a period of time when I was real isolated, and the only friends I really had were the gay friends I knew at the bar. I mean it was like bar friends, you know, and that was it."

Cutting oneself off from the bar is not easily done. If a man makes a clean break with the bars, he may very well estrange himself from his bar-based support group and find that he is completely on his own. The men who have been able to successfully break with bar life report that leaving was facilitated by meeting gay people in other social contexts such as gay centers, parties, the Metropolitan Community Church, school, by meeting them through other friends, or by expanding acquaintances made in the bar to other social settings. When men establish friendships that are not tied to the bars, they find that they have less time for bar visits and that other recreational activities are more attractive. Those men who have left the bar often state that a wider social life or having a bigger variety of friends has freed them from having to rely on the bar scene for emotional support and social activities.

While much of the interaction that goes on in gay bars is not significantly different from that described by ethnographers who have studied other kinds of drinking establishments, the meaning of the gay bar is different for its habitués. The bar is a focal point for gay men, around which they organize their lives. It functions for gay men as a place to find role models, normalize a "deviant" sexual orientation, and reduce the feeling of being stigmatized that they experience daily in the larger society.

5. Love Relationships and Drinking

Steven and Bill's house sits at the end of a narrow road that winds its way upward through a forest of eucalyptus trees. A small, shaggy, rusty black Hungarian Puli ambles out of the shade to greet visitors. Several cats of various hues roam the grounds. The house is low and rambling, surrounded by citrus and avocado trees, birds of paradise, and flowering bushes. The view, overlooking much of southern Paradise County, is spectacular.

Inside, the house is comfortable and lived-in. Steven and Bill are renovating; they have just finished replacing the kitchen floor and cabinets. The house has no central heating, and the large living room, painted mauve, is dominated by a stone fireplace. The room is filled with curios, antiques, and Aztec artifacts. Steven says,

> Well, we do live a more gracious lifestyle, and I'm not afraid to admit it because we do enjoy the finer things in life. You look about our house, we don't have an average house. How many statues brought straight from Italy do you find in a house? How many walls this color do you find in a house? How many houses do you find furniture like this in?

Steven and Bill have been together for four and a half years. They met at the Metropolitan Community Church, but they did not feel a mutual attraction at first. As Bill says, "The two of us turned each other off." Steven had been in two prior gay relationships, neither of which lasted more than a year. Bill has been heterosexually married twice and has two grown daughters. Although he has lived with a couple of other men before Steven, this is the first time he has been in a Holy Union, a relationship sanctioned by the Metropolitan Community Church.

Their relationship has not always been smooth. There are two sensitive areas mentioned by both partners: finances and their age difference of twenty-five years. Bill says, "Steven is piss poor when it comes to handling money. He can't handle fifteen cents. And it's probably the one point in our association that causes the most problems, money. Because we are really living beyond our means." The power differential between Bill and Steven underlies these conflicts. After having lived together for over two years, Steven packed up and left. "Up until that point," he says, "I never felt that I was given the right to make any decisions, and if I did they were wrong. . . . The culmination was to tell Bill goodbye. . . . I think I surprised him, because he didn't think I was capable of doing something like this." The separation lasted only a week, but Steven feels that it served to develop mutual respect. Bill confirms Steven's feeling when he notes, "Sure we have our arguments, but we're always capable of sitting down and talking about it. . . . I'm twenty-five years older than Steven and I've had a lot more living and a lot more experience than he's had, and I hope that he is learning from me, [but] I'm learning from him, too. He's as much a help to me as I am to him."

Steven and Bill rarely go out to bars. They do, however, drink at home every evening. They also have friends over for dinner—Bill is a gourmet cook—and drinking is an integral part of the occasion. "Booze is always offered at a party," Steven says.

> I don't know if we do it because it's a fact of life or what. But we have it and we're going to share it . . . and about 95% of the friends that we have probably have the same shared feelings as we do about alcohol. . . . They know how to drink, they know they like to drink, they're not coming along just to take stock of the inventory and drink up as much as they want.

Their choice of gay friends, according to Steven, is "very, very select and very, very minimal. Most gays make us sick." A few gay couples, their closest friends, have been together twenty or thirty years. Most of the other gay couples they know have been together for only a year or two. The majority of their gay friends are single, and about half of their friendships are with heterosexual couples and families. When they have guests, Bill and Steven prefer mixed groups of heterosexual couples, gay couples, and gay singles.

While Steven says that he has been drinking more since he and Bill became a couple, Bill claims that his own alcohol consumption has actually decreased. His own preference is wine and cocktails, but he notes that Steven drinks a lot of beer: "He can really pour the beer away, and it doesn't seem to have any effect on him whatsoever. For instance, he'll come home from work and he'll drink four or five cans of beer as opposed to my one." Yet Bill feels that Steven is able to handle his alcohol use. "If it were creating a problem for him, then I would definitely be concerned."

Although the bar scene is the most visible and probably the most important setting in which drinking occurs, it is by no means the only one. Some men drink at home, either alone or with a small, select group of friends. Sometimes, like Steven and Bill, they become involved in a love relationship, establish a household, and develop a private social life. Although these men may not be bar habitués, this does not necessarily mean that alcohol is unimportant to them. On the contrary, drinking is well integrated into the lives of many gay couples. Thus, a more complete picture of alcohol use among gay men requires an understanding of its place in their private worlds. I turn, then, to an examination of drinking behavior among gay men who are involved in intimate relationships, focusing not only on how gay couples use alcohol, but also, and more importantly, on the ways in which love relationships affect, and are affected by, drinking.

Drinking Behavior among Gay Couples

Having been in a love relationship was a common experience for the men in this study. Ten of them were in such a relationship at the time they were interviewed, and eighteen others had had a lover in the past. Eight of the ten men who were currently in a love relationship were living with their lovers.[1]

Drinking was an important part of the lifestyles of most of the couples in the study. It was part of their daily routine. For example, the men might come home from work, mix a drink or pour a beer, and sit down and unwind from the day's events, discussing what had happened on the job. Or, they might have wine with dinner or an after-dinner drink later on: "I'll get home and while I'm fixing dinner he'll fix us a drink. We have a drink before dinner and then after dinner we fix a drink. And we just sit down and watch TV or read or play games" (Erik). Some couples define drinking as part of an "elegant" lifestyle. Since it is an accompaniment to "gracious living," they do not necessarily consider themselves to be excessive drinkers, even if they are drinking every day. Steven, for example, described how alcohol is integrated into his life:

> Well, definitely every night when Bill comes home, we'll have a couple of drinks, sit around, and yak over the mail. Then we're ready for dinner, and . . . we always have wine every . . . dinner. . . . Then, once in awhile in the evening after dinner, it's enjoyable to sit down to what I call my private stock—it's Christian Brothers' brandy or Benedictine cognac. Almaden is another favorite of mine. That's just a normal routine in our lives and in our household, and I've often wondered if it is a habit, and I really think that it is not a habit because it is something that we enjoy doing very, very much. . . . It's also—this is an egotistical way of looking at it—it's also part of the act that people in-the-know do. Most people, your average American, say, husband and wife and four kids, they're certainly not going to be drinking cocktails before dinner. . . . I'm not saying we're better than they are, but we have taken one of these more enjoyable parts of the higher society into our own lives and enjoyed it equally.[2]

The social lives of the two men quoted above and their lovers revolve mainly around their homes and include other couples or single friends who come over to dinner or to play cards or other games. Under these circumstances, drinking is a feature of an evening's home entertainment, a phenomenon first noted by Warren (1974), who emphasized the importance of social drinking at home, especially for older men. While younger gays do a lot of their socializing in bars, she notes: "routine home entertaining is the mainstay of the middle-aged, middle-class secret gay community. . . . The invitation may be for cocktails only, or, more usually, for cocktails and dinner" (p. 49). Bill illustrates how he integrates alcohol use into home entertainments:

> I kind of put drinking as a component part of entertaining; not that people should get drunk, I don't mean it in that sense, but I think

it's just conducive to people getting along well with each other. I don't know if it oils their tongues or what. . . . Whenever we entertain, I'll have a drink with whoever comes to visit. We had a couple over the night before last for dinner, and we had martinis before the meal and we had wine with dinner. And then we all got to playing "Aggravation" at the dinner table, and after we were done we had a little thimble glass of Irish Mist, but we don't very often have anything to drink after a meal, except coffee.

A number of men in this study have a lifestyle similar to that of Bill and Steven. They often own suburban homes and live much like the middle-class heterosexual couples in their neighborhoods. Only rarely do they go to gay bars; when this happens it is usually for specific reasons such as to celebrate birthdays or anniversaries or to shoot pool. Bill, for instance, reported having reluctantly taken Steven and some friends to a gay bar as part of a dinner celebration. "And I was bored stiff with the whole damn thing," he said. "I had one drink while I was there. I was just glad to get out of the place." Erik noted that he and his lover, Frank, only go to bars when they want to shoot pool and that he almost never drinks anything stronger than cola while he is there. He and Frank had just bought a new house and could not afford to spend their money in a bar.

In general, being in a love relationship tended to reduce bar visitation for the men in the study. Half of those respondents who had experienced such a relationship reported that being intimately involved with someone decreased their bar-going behavior, while only three men stated that their attendance had increased.[3] This does not differentiate gay pairs from heterosexual couples. Cosper et al. (1987), for instance, found that only 29% of married people in their sample had a regular drinking place, compared to 54% of singles and 49% of those who were separated or divorced. In their multivariate analysis of factors involved in having a regular drinking place, they discovered that "marital status is virtually as strong a predictor of regularity as is drinking; unmarried people are more likely to be regulars at drinking establishments" (p. 256). Similarly, Fisher (1981) found that "married respondents were less likely to be tavern users" (p. 44). The same relationship has also been noted by Clark (1981).

There are several reasons why gay men who are in love relationships tend to reduce the frequency of their bar visits. The most obvious of these is that the gay bar is a sexual marketplace. Many men, therefore, stay clear of the bar world for fear that they will be tempted into other liaisons, thus jeopardizing their love relationship:

> If we were to frequent bars, we would start having problems at home. We know this based on other people's lives and we know it based on our lives the few times we have gone to bars. All kinds of problems can come to a couple who start spending a lot of their time in bars, instead of at home with each other, working on their own lives. (Steven)

Bars can be disruptive influences for heterosexual couples as well. A recent study of adjustment to husband-wife interaction by wives of alcoholics found this to be the case (Weinberg & Vogler, 1990). According to one woman, "He never had room in his life for us—the only people who ever mattered to him were barfly friends." Another woman said, "I always used to feel left out, so I would join him at the bar. Now, I no longer drink."[4]

Despite the fact that bars can serve as sexual meeting places for heterosexuals (Cavan, 1966; Prus, 1983; Roebuck & Spray, 1967), sexual infidelity linked to bars did not seem to be an issue for the wives in the study. One woman did say, "I am afraid he will leave me—divorce me for a younger, prettier woman," but she was in the minority. Only a few women (17%) shared this specific fear.

Some gay men do not go to bars, not because they fear jealousy or competition, but simply because they find their sexual and emotional needs met within their relationship. Or, as in the case of Erik and his partner, a change to a coupled lifestyle may affect spending patterns, so that money that had formerly been spent in the bars is now needed to pay mortgages and related expenses. Finally, two men said that they did not frequent bars because their lovers were not old enough to go with them.[5]

The Effects of Love Relationships on Drinking

Being in a love relationship reduces bar visitation, but does not necessarily mean that drinking is thereby reduced as well. There are a number of ways a relationship can affect drinking, and for some couples alcohol use is simply shifted to the home without any concomitant moderation. In other cases, drinking can either decrease or increase. There can be changes in the amount consumed at any given time, and in the number and kinds of occasions during which alcohol is used. The place where drinking occurs, the amount of time spent in drinking situations, the type of beverage used, and the meaning of drinking for the individual are all subject to change.

In order to assess the effect of relationships on alcohol use, the men were first asked the general question, How do your love relationships affect your drinking? If the respondent did not include information on changes in the quantity or frequency of consumption in his answer, he was asked more specifically, Do you drink more or less when you are involved in a relationship with someone? The information derived from the responses to these two questions suggests that when a person changes his drinking habits as a result of being in a love relationship, he most often reduces the amount of alcohol consumed. Thirteen men said that they drank less when they were part of a couple and six others claimed that their alcohol use increased.[6] Changes in the frequency of alcohol use correlate strongly with changes in the amount consumed.

Increases in Alcohol Consumption

Under what conditions do relationships cause alcohol use to increase? In most instances, an individual increases his own drinking if his lover is a heavy drinker. Often, that lover is older than he and may teach him how to order drinks and how to consume them, and even how to know which drinks are proper in particular settings. For example, Steven is twenty-nine and Bill is fifty-four. When he first met Bill, Steven had been frequenting bars for a number of years, yet he was a comparatively light drinker and, in his own estimation, ignorant about alcohol consumption.

TOM: Has your drinking style changed?
STEVEN: Tremendously. I know booze now. I know drinks. I know wine. And I drink it because I appreciate it, and I enjoy it.
TOM: How do you account for these changes?
STEVEN: Maturity. Plus Bill. Bill has taught me an awful lot about life. . . . I became a serious drinker when I met Bill, because I started to understand what I was drinking. . . . When I was by myself, before I met Bill, I didn't have any booze in the house. And I've often thought about this. I'd occasionally have a six-pack of beer, but I never had any hard liquor or wine.

Similarly, Weinberg and Vogler (1990) found that women married to alcoholics were naive about alcohol and alcoholism when they first met their spouses. Forty-nine percent of these wives were totally ignorant about drinking, and 40% had only some information. Like the gay men in the present sample, they also began drinking with their spouses (46% had drunk with their husbands in the past, and an additional 27% were still drinking with them at the time of the research). They were, however, comparatively light drinkers themselves; none of them consumed more than three drinks on a given occasion (46% had one or two drinks).

Another situation in which a lighter drinker increased his consumption to match that of a lover occurred when the lover was a bartender in a gay establishment. Respondents often described these lovers as having been alcoholic:

> I was really drinking heavy, and when Larry and I were together I was drunk, I suppose, more evenings than not. If you go to the bars when you're a bartender's spouse, or when you're a bartender, you drink for free. People buy you drinks, encourage you to drink, and you're supposed to be encouraging them to drink, 'cause that's where the bar makes its money. And you have to drink with them if that's what it takes to get them to drink. And I really started having as much of a problem as he did. Until then I never figured he had a problem. I was so oblivious to alcoholism, I guess, that I didn't realize I was married to an alcoholic and so . . . I faced it in me. I realized that's where I was headed. (Michael)

Eventually, Michael stopped using alcohol. His lover, however, did not, and this caused the end of their relationship.

Decreases in Alcohol Consumption

As I have already noted, when involvement in a love relationship altered a respondent's drinking behavior, it most often reduced his alcohol consumption. It was, however, unusual for a heavy drinker to reduce his intake. Only two men who were heavy drinkers had done so, and in neither case did this seem to be a dramatic reduction. Both men continued to visit bars. Interestingly, they both attributed the decline in their drinking to feeling secure and loved in a relationship. Ted, for example, said that when he was with his lover, "we had other things to do. . . . I could sit home with him and just snuggle up in front of the fireplace and watch TV and not drink. . . . I can get the relaxed feeling, that thing that I was looking for in alcohol, [from] being with someone." Bruce noted, "When I could find somebody that cared enough for me, I usually drank less." More frequently, when one member of a pair reduced his drinking to match that of a lover, it was either because his own drinking was not inordinately heavy, or because his lover's drinking was not significantly lighter than his own. For instance, Tim, who is a light drinker, stopped drinking because his lover did not drink very much: "Well, this one [lover] didn't like drinking that much . . . and that's one of the reasons why I stopped, 'cause he just didn't drink. If he had been a drinker, I probably would have drunk right along with him."

I have shown that being in an intimate relationship tends to reduce bar visitation but does not necessarily reduce drinking, which may simply continue at home. This appears to be especially true if the men are heavy drinkers prior to the relationship. One man said,

> When I first came to Paradise City, I was living with a lover for a year and we didn't go out; maybe twice in the whole year we went out. We stayed home and drank viciously. So I guess the amount really didn't change, whether I went to a bar or not. But he was an alcoholic, too, so we just drank up a storm together. (Chuck)

For at least some men, however, drinking was reduced precisely because they reduced their bar activities: "When I was engaged with a lover, we didn't go out to the bars so much because he was extremely jealous, so we mostly drank at home. That moderated my drinking when I was with [him] (Joel)."

The Effects of Drinking on Love Relationships

Up to this point, I have been concerned with the effect of love relationships on drinking, although there have been some implicit references made to the ways excessive drinking may affect interaction between a couple. For example, I noted in passing that the alcoholism of Michael's partner caused the dissolution of their relationship. Here, however, I shall be examining more explicitly the impact of drinking on gay love relationships.

Nardi (1982a) has pointed out that there are a number of unique characteristics of gay love relationships that may tend to make them more vulnerable to the potentially destructive effects of heavy drinking. He notes that clearly defined roles, which are traditionally based on gender in heterosexual relationships, are lacking in gay relationships. This lack of structure may "lead to more conflicts revolving around power and equality issues" (p. 86) than might occur between heterosexual couples. In addition, he emphasizes that "the absence of legal and social norms regulating gay relationships often makes it easier to create one's own rules and roles while also making it easier to dissolve relationships when problems arise. How the gay subculture regulates and supports intimate relationships will have an impact on a couple's responses to alcohol abuse" (p. 86).

Nardi's observations are well illustrated in the histories of many of the men in the present study. Some of them noted that the lack of a clear definition of roles in their relationships led to problems of power:

> In all my relationships, I didn't have equal respect. I was either more wifely or more husbandly, one way or the other in almost a traditional sense. And I like more of an equal thing, where you can be different from one another as well as very similar in some ways. [In one relationship] I felt I was the dominant big brother, head of household, [and I had to] decide everything. That was so repulsive to me, I thought, "I don't want anybody assimilating themselves to my life and I don't want to assimilate myself to someone else's life. It made me look very realistically at [those relationships]. (Michael)

Michael reported having had two important relationships. In the first of these, his lover was a bartender in a gay establishment and a heavy user of alcohol. In the early stages of the relationship, which lasted more than two years, his lover was the dominant force, and Michael found his own alcohol consumption increasing. Eventually realizing that both he and his lover had a drinking problem, Michael quit. Part of his reason for deciding not to drink was that he resented being dominated in the relationship and was attempting to regain some control over his situation. He said, "Part of it was . . . just downright opposition to my lover, too. I think that was part of it. Do something to make him mad. There was a lot going on there. It was a very volatile and unhealthy relationship. It was amazing it lasted the couple of years it did." At that point, his abstinence and his lover's heavy drinking "became an obstacle in our relationship." His lover resented Michael's decision not to drink and retaliated by trying to make him feel guilty and uncomfortable for not drinking. Slowly, the dominance order in the relationship began to shift, with Michael becoming the unwilling primary force. His lover became dependent on him, confessed his failings, and asked for forgiveness. The same sorts of shifts also occur within heterosexual marriages. Jackson (1954) describes stages in family adjustment to an alcoholic member and labels these shifts as attempts to reorganize in spite of the problem. At this point, the spouse is eased out of his family roles, and the wife, just like Michael, becomes the manager of the home and the decision maker.

Michael's relationship reached a climax when this lover induced him to become the "master" in a sadomasochistic sexual fantasy. His drinking seemed to moderate as long as Michael controlled the situation and participated in sadomasochistic games, but "I definitely wasn't any master. . . . I played the part and it seemed to help him overcome the alcohol. The alcohol abuse went way down for awhile." Eventually, however, even this symbolic control ceased to work. His lover's drinking increased, and the relationship broke up.

Michael reported that his second love relationship involved the opposite problem. From the start, he was the leader of the couple. This new man "lived his life totally adjusted to mine," he said. "I was very uncomfortable with that." His lover's dependency extended to alcohol use as well: "He drank when I drank. And I drank when I felt like I had to for social acceptance, and so he followed suit." This relationship also ended, but for reasons other than alcohol use.

The kind of power struggles mentioned by Nardi (1982a) and described by Michael were not uncommon in the coupled histories of the men in the study. Often they emerged over the issue of alcohol use: one member of the pair attempted to restrict or encourage his partner's drinking. The other man dealt with this either by hiding his consumption from his lover by sneaking out to the bars, or by confronting the partner quite forcefully with the disputed drinking in an attempt to clarify the rules and set limits on the other's control of his behavior. Robert's experience illustrates both ways of dealing with a partner's attempts to control one's alcohol use. In the beginning of the relationship he was cautiously feeling his way, but as it evolved, the issue of who had the right to control whose behavior came to the forefront:

> I used to have somewhat of a problem when I was living with my lover because he was very much opposed to alcohol. He never even touched a drop in his life, and he used to get down on me once in awhile for having a drink. . . . Early in our relationship, like the first year or so I wouldn't drink around him. . . . [Later] I began again drinking in his presence and he would complain about it, but I'd go right ahead, and in the latter part of our relationship I could drink in front of him and he wouldn't say anything.

Drinking itself was not of crucial importance. Robert claimed that although "his response [to my drinking] was very negative, it didn't have any real affect on our staying together." Rather, the real issue was that "his argument against it was reasonable for himself, but I didn't believe it was right for him to deny my right to drink."

Although Robert perceived his lover's responses as an unfair attempt to control his behavior and reacted accordingly, this may not have been the man's intention at all. He simply may have been motivated by concern about the potentially harmful effects of drinking on someone about whom he cared very much. Some of the respondents in this study said that their primary reason for confronting a lover whom they saw as being too involved in alcohol use was their fear for his health and safety. They acted on this fear in several ways, some of which are similar to the kinds of interactive patterns described by Wiseman (1980) in her discussion of the home treatment used by wives of alcoholics. They would try logical arguments and persuasion:

> I just was honest with him. I just said, "You drink too much. I don't enjoy going out and getting blown away all the time, and it's not fun, it's not acceptable, it's not healthy, it's not productive, it just isn't in my system of values." And then he'd try to talk me out of it, you know, and say, well, "That's not being very [much] fun." (Gregory)

They would plead and threaten to leave:

> The relationship got to the point where it was intolerable as it was, and it was either that his drinking was going to decrease and his drunk behavior in general was going to decrease, or I was going to leave. (Gregory)

They would use indirect methods in the hope of encouraging the lover to reduce his drinking:

> I was a teetotaler most of the previous year [before we broke up] because once I realized he had an alcohol problem I figured that my quitting drinking might encourage him to do the same. I didn't need to quit drinking that much for myself, and at that point, I must say, I did it for him. (Michael)

As Wiseman (1980) has shown, power struggles revolving around the use of alcohol are also found in heterosexual relationships. One wife of an alcoholic (Weinberg & Vogler, 1990) had been in a situation similar to to Michael's. She said, "I was too easygoing. If I was a domineering person and voiced my dislike of his behavior . . . that only made matters worse; he'd become abusive." Another woman said, "I resented the responsibilities I felt I handled alone."[7] One difference between the gay men in the present study and the female spouses in other research studies (Weinberg & Vogler, 1990; Wiseman, 1980) is that the latter drank with their husbands as an indirect strategy to control their alcohol use, while the former began by drinking heavily with their lovers, and their realization that there was an alcohol problem grew out of their drinking together. Some of the men thought that alcohol use precipitated fights and impeded effective communication. In a circular fashion, these fights contributed to the breakup of their relationships, which, in turn, served to increase alcohol consumption.

Dealing with the alcohol problems of a lover is complicated by another factor. Gay couples do not live in a vacuum. They are usually involved in networks of friends or extended families. These groups, which often form around drinking situations, encourage and normalize heavy alcohol use (Nardi, 1982a), and this makes it very difficult to break away from drinking or to encourage one's lover to do so. For example, Gregory found that his best efforts to influence his heavily drinking lover to reduce his alcohol consumption were continually being undermined by others, who resented him for his own efforts at sobriety:

> My last lover . . . was a heavy drinker, a definite problem drinker, and most of his friends were also. And I was uncomfortable with that, and I tended to avoid whenever possible going out with them,

which bothered him a lot. . . . And all his friends would get angry, you know, like, "Oh, God, what are you putting up with that for?". . . . I'd resist [drinking], his plying me with [alcohol], or his friends' [pressure]. I'd just say, "no, thank you," which, of course, made them hostile. It was like, "Gee, who are you not to drink with us? What's your problem?"

Another problem making it difficult to confront an alcoholic lover is that when a relationship ends, friends often choose sides, so that one may become isolated from former associates. Thus, one man said that all of his contacts with other gays had been made through his lover, and that after they broke up, his lover's friends blamed him for the other man's increased alcohol consumption. He therefore felt compelled to withdraw from the bar scene, with a consequent loss of his social circle.

Since alcohol use is ubiquitous in the gay world, it affects couples as well as single men. Although bar attendance appeared to have been reduced by being involved in a love relationship, this did not necessarily mean that the men in this study moderated their drinking. Drinking could be increased through involvement with an older, more sophisticated lover, a partner who was a bartender, or as a result of stresses within the relationship. On the other hand, heavy drinking itself is often encouraged, or at least not discouraged, by one's associates, and may lead to the dissolution of a couple.

In many ways, the situation of gay men in long-term love relationships is similar to that of heterosexually married couples. In both cases, issues of control become intertwined with those of alcohol use. Both gays and heterosexuals often become enablers, facilitating the very behavior that causes problems within their relationships. Both become frustrated, anxious, and utilize similar strategies to control their mates' drinking. In neither case is the spouse/lover usually successful. At some point, just as the gay men report, women married to problem drinkers also give up and try to detach themselves from their husbands' drinking (Jackson, 1954, 1962; Weinberg & Vogler, 1990), and the relationship may dissolve. Forty-six percent of Weinberg and Vogler's (1990) sample, for example, reported having separated as a result of alcohol problems.

One difference between gays and heterosexuals in similar circumstances may be the social support available to them as they are going through a crisis. None of the men in the present study reported receiving such help; there are few institutionalized supports for gay couples in crisis, especially in the case of alcohol problems (Whitney, 1982). For heterosexual couples, on the other hand, there are not only familial and formal organizations to which they may eventually turn (Jackson, 1954) but also specialized support groups such as Alanon. Weinberg and Vogler (1990) found that Alanon was crucial in helping the alcoholics' wives cope with their husbands' drinking.

6. Drinking Careers

One way of understanding the drinking histories of the men in this study is by using the concept of "career" as an organizing device. First developed in the study of occupations, the career model "takes into account the fact that patterns of behavior *develop* [Becker's italics] in orderly sequence" (Becker, 1963, p. 23). The concept of career implies not only a sequential involvement in a pattern of behavior, but it also assumes that "the explanation of each step is thus a part of the explanation of the resulting behavior" (p. 23).[1] Yet careers do not necessarily follow a smooth and uninterrupted course. There are often static periods, vacillations, reversals, and other changes in direction. For instance, some of the lighter drinkers I spoke to report having been heavily involved in alcohol use at one time. They never defined themselves as alcoholics or problem drinkers, however, and they eventually reduced their drinking. These men will be discussed in chapter 7. A number of other studies note the problematic nature of careers. Ray (1961), for instance, has shown that heroin addicts go through cycles of abstinence and heroin use, whose fluctuations are accounted for by the ways the individual interprets his or her interactions with other people. Similar observations have been made of alcoholics (Wiseman, 1970, 1979) and men attempting to deal with a suspected homosexual identity (Weinberg, 1983, 1984).

In a study of the moral career of the mental patient, Goffman (1959) used a phenomenological approach, attempting "to take the patient's point of view" (p. 123). His concern was with "the *moral* [Goffman's italics] aspects of career—that is, the regular sequence of changes that career entails in the person's self and in his framework of imagery for judging himself and others" (p. 123). I use Goffman's

73

emphasis in this chapter—that is, although I will be examining the development of drinking behavior, I am most interested in the individual's perceptions of himself, his drinking, his own responses, and the feedback he obtains from significant others.

Apart from the physical changes that sometimes accompany the advancement of a career, there are usually alterations in self-concept. Sometimes this involves a transformation of identity. The individual must conceptualize his or her behavior as symbolic of the underlying pattern, status, or identity indicated by this behavior (Weinberg, 1978, 1983). For example, for people to think of themselves as alcoholics, they must come to understand their drinking behavior (among many other factors) as part of and reflective of an alcoholic identity. Matza (1969) refers to this as the "special relationship between being and doing" (p. 170). As the literature indicates, more is involved in careers than merely engaging in specific acts. Such behavior may become elaborated into a way of life, culminating in a new identity or master status (Becker, 1963) used by individuals and others as a means of organizing their perceptions and consequent actions.

The men in this study represent a wide variety of drinking styles and adjustments, from those who are almost teetotalers to individuals who are heavy drinkers to men who are abstinent alcoholics. Some men stop in a gay bar for an occasional beer and to find out what is going on in the gay community, while others organize their lives around the bars and are in them every day of the week. Some men use alcohol to enhance a social occasion such as a dinner out, while others use alcohol instrumentally to cope with stress and unhappiness. The following descriptions illustrate the diversity of alcohol involvement among gay men.

Vinnie is a recovering alcoholic. He began drinking at age twelve. His beverage of choice in those days was wine. "I was guzzling it," he remembers. "I was drinking exorbitant amounts of it. Right from the bottle, as a matter of fact." By the time he first went to a gay bar at age twenty-two, Vinnie was drinking heavily, "maybe an average of ten to fifteen drinks a night. On the weekends, maybe a little more." He went to the bars about three times a week, "basically to drink." Social contacts and even cruising were secondary. Over the next two years, his pace of drinking increased. He began going to the bars at 5:00 or 6:00 in the evening, having already consumed a six-pack of beer, and he would stay until they closed at 2:00 A.M.

When I asked him, What do you feel were your own needs that the bars were helping to fill?, he replied, "Loneliness. Without a doubt, that's the first [need]. And it was a warm place to drink, a place to be around people and drink."

After a time, Vinnie consciously avoided interacting with others in the bar. "I'd just generally drink by myself in the corner and pass out," he said. Right before he stopped drinking he was consuming four or five quarts of beer a day. "I would drink as much as I could handle all the time," he noted. "And when I'd pass out I'd wake up and continue to drink." During his last six months of drinking, he isolated himself at home. "It was easier and less expensive to drink at home. I felt so bad about myself, I had such low self-worth that I couldn't face people, so I naturally stayed at home." Vinnie's heavy drinking precipitated a crisis:

> I was in a train station in San Francisco, I remember, and I couldn't decide whether to take the train north or the train south. And I just sat down in the middle of the station and started to cry, because I realized that it was sort of symbolic of everything I had ever tried to do. I couldn't do anything anymore. I couldn't function anymore. I couldn't think or feel anything. So I called up the hospital. I knew I had a drinking problem, and it took me a year to stop, to finally stop altogether.

Larry is sixty-eight years old. He came out only three years ago. He does not drink very much: "Maybe once a month would be a pretty good average," he estimated. His drinking experience is very limited. "I suppose I had a taste of wine or something when I was in my twenties," he told me. "There was never any alcohol around my home as I was growing up, not that my parents were against it—it just wasn't a part of things." Larry cannot stand the smell or taste of beer, but he does occasionally drink wine. "I can enjoy a glass of good wine with a meal, though that's not a regular practice. . . . If we have guests for dinner and I serve wine, I may have some then. With no guests, there'd be no wine. It's not a regular habit," he reported. Larry has never been drunk, but, he said, "I've had enough at times that I feel the slightest little light-headedness, and maybe a little flush, but that's all."

On a few occasions, Larry has gone to gay bars. However, he sees the bars as more appropriate for younger men, and not being much of a drinker, he feels out of place. When I asked him whether he would ever go again, he replied, "Not on my own. Somebody would have to encourage me to go along. Then I would be bored all the time I was there."

Larry's social life is centered around the Metropolitan Community Church and the friends he has made there. "My contact with the church is not just the church service, necessarily, because it is a very active church. Something's always happening: social activities or an affair at the beach, or a picnic, or what-have-you." Clearly, alcohol is not a very important part of Larry's life.

Frank began drinking in the Navy. "Yeah," he stated, "I did a lot. The clubs on base, mainly. You know, like when I was on the ship. We'd go over there at night, Christ, and drink ourselves into oblivion. And when we were in port we'd go into town. . . . That was our primary form of recreation." He started going to gay bars just before he turned twenty-nine. During the three to five hours he spent in bars, he would drink five to eight beers. Now, he said, he is drinking less, although he still drinks every day. He and his lover have two or three drinks at home during an evening. Before they bought their new house, he told me, "We'd get out periodically, maybe once a week, go out for dinner, and we'd have maybe a drink before dinner and a drink with it or after." They went to the bars two or three times a week. In the bars, they now rarely drink anything stronger than diet soft drinks. Frank said, "We go now primarily to shoot pool—well, we don't go to meet people and we don't go to socialize. . . . The primary objective when we go is to shoot pool." Recently, their trips to the bar have "practically disappeared."

Robert began drinking in a regular way at the age of eighteen, right after high school. Friends who were of drinking age would purchase beer, and then they would have an informal party at someone's home. He started going to gay bars at the age of twenty-three, shortly after he came out. At that time, he was going about once a week with a friend from work. He usually drank a single beer, and "probably not more than three." "Now when I go out to bars, I seldom drink alcohol," he said. "I may have one alcoholic beverage. If I go out to a bar that has two-for-one night, I may have a beer or two. Other than that, most of the time that I go to gay bars now, I get a nonalcoholic beverage such as mineral water or juice. I don't really care for drinking that much anymore . . . in the bar." His current drinking is not much different from when he first came out, except that he prefers White Russians to beer.

Robert has a "small, select group" of friends, whom he met through Lutherans Concerned and Dignity.[2] He also meets people through his participation in the gay center and through mutual friends. He goes to bars either with them or by himself, depending on how he feels at the time. His favorite establishments, Gunsmoke and the Pacific Coast, are dance bars. He also goes to the Cabin, a bar near his home. The bars are important to Robert because they give him a sense of belonging: "Being in that community, with my own people, its own culture, it's very much a part of gay life. I would say the majority of gay people in urban areas go to bars." He goes to meet people. "I just enjoy the atmosphere," he said. Robert also drinks at parties, usually one or two glasses of wine, but he drinks the most when he goes out to dinner.

Early Alcohol Use

The men in this study began using alcohol in a consistent way at the median age of eighteen (with a range of twelve to sixty). This generally preceded both their coming out (median age of nineteen with a range of eleven to forty-two) and their first visit to a gay bar (median age of twenty-one with a range of fifteen to sixty-five).

For the most part, the early drinking experiences of these men were little different from those of most young people;[3] all but two of them began drinking in social situations. In some cases, alcohol use began with friends in the neighborhood, in high school, or in college. For others, alcohol use did not begin until they left home. For example, some men did not begin to drink until they were in the military, while others started using alcohol with adult friends, lovers, or, in one case, a spouse.

When they first began drinking, few of the men were concerned about developing alcohol-related problems. Only five of them were fearful about the meaning of their drinking. Two of the five were also ambivalent because they had parents who had died of alcoholism. One of these men has developed ulcers and other illnesses over the course of many years of alcohol use. A third man, Chris, currently identifies himself as a recovering (i.e., nondrinking) alcoholic. He began drinking at the age of nineteen, while he was in the service and stationed in Europe. In that social context, he says, "I could drink and it was considered okay to become sloppy drunk periodically. It was part of that thing I was in, in the service in Germany, and it was accepted behavior." However, these norms, which protect many men from having to define themselves as problem drinkers, did not serve that purpose for very long in his case:

> TOM: How did you feel about drinking at that point?
> CHRIS: I thought I was an alcoholic. I had always based my drinking on the [condition] that if I ever drank as badly as my father and experienced some of the things that my father had done, I wouldn't drink. I can remember in Germany one time. . . . I woke up clutching the toilet, with vomit all over my suit, all over me, and just a total mess . . . and a similar incident had happened to my father in my childhood and I thought that was disgusting. And when it happened to me I recognized it as something that had happened previously to him. And I was shocked, and for a long time I didn't drink. For a long time I monitored it very carefully, and for a long time I didn't have the problem.

Unlike Chris and a few others, most of the men either enjoyed drinking or did not think about it at all. Kevin said, for example, "It was a big deal," and Alan recalled, "I thought it was real cool because nobody else did." This category includes four of six self-identified recovering alcoholics and two of four self-identified alcoholics who were still drinking. When asked about their initial feelings about drinking, a number of men echoed Erik, who said, "I don't really think I had any opinion about it. It was just a part of the routine, as it probably is now. Only one time did I ever feel that I was drinking too much, and so I backed off."

A few men reported that they had disliked alcohol when they first began to use it. They continued to drink, however, because of social pressures:

> I never really liked it, but you were supposed to do it. If you were in a bar, you had to have a drink. I mean, you can't order milk, you know. (Sully)

> I didn't like it at all. I didn't like the taste of the alcohol, I didn't like what it did to me, but it seemed to help me get to know people

or meet people and be more accepted by maybe a certain group of people, so I did [it] anyway. (Mark)

Finally, one man drank because he felt he needed alcohol to relieve school pressures. Five others failed to answer the question.

When they were first learning to drink, most of the men preferred mixed drinks (37%), beer (26%), or a combination of beer and mixed drinks (14%). A few men used wine (7%), combinations of beer and wine (4%), wine and mixed drinks (4%), or all three kinds of alcoholic drinks (4%). Two men (4%) did not respond to the question. The number of drinks consumed by the respondents at any given time varied widely. Nine percent of the men had only one drink, 28% consumed two or three beverages, 13% had four or five drinks, and 31% took six or more drinks during a drinking episode. Two men said that they could not remember how much they drank but that it was "quite a bit," and seven men did not answer the question.

Family Influences

Several men began to drink with parents or other family members. Usually, in these cases, adolescent children were permitted to have a little wine with dinner, or a beer during a family cookout. The men did not think this was unusual behavior, and it had no negative consequences: "In my family it was natural," Hal told me. Sully said, "I guess alcohol was never all that big a thing, because my parents were really open about it." It was not used excessively, nor was much fuss made about it. For some men, however, drinking in the family was a weekly routine encouraged by their parents:

> My parents are alcoholics, and my mom usually wanted somebody to party with. So she had me skip Mondays in school when I was . . . in the tenth and eleventh grades and go out with her every Sunday night and just get bombed. So when I was about fourteen or fifteen, I was drinking every Sunday night. (Alan)

> I can remember when I was in high school, Dad used to get me out of bed like at 2:00 in the morning on probably a once-a-week basis, and he'd want somebody to have a drink with him. And he'd wake me up out of a sound sleep. (P. J.)

The situations reported by the men quoted above were not unique. Almost two-thirds of the men I interviewed reported that at least one parent had had problems with alcohol. In six cases, both parents were defined as alcoholics. One man reported that his mother had died from alcoholism, while another respondent said that his father was currently dying from alcohol-related illnesses. Additionally, one-third of the men said that their siblings were alcoholics. These are higher figures than those reported in studies of samples of hetero-sexuals.[4]

As noted in chapter 4, only six of the men began drinking in gay bars, so apparently, while this institution is critical for encouraging and sustaining alcohol use, it is relatively unimportant as a site for initial drinking.

Consequences of Drinking

The gay community does not often label a person as a problem drinker, since gays use such a wide latitude in determining unacceptable drinking-related behavior (Warren, 1974). As noted in chapter 3, fewer than one-third of the men reported having been told by others that they had a drinking problem. The proportion of men who had been more publicly labeled was even smaller. Ten men said that they had been stopped by the police after having been drinking. Nine of these offenses were for "driving under the influence" (referred to as "5-0-2s" in Paradise City), and only once did the officer fail to make an arrest. In this case, the respondent barely managed to pass a roadside agility test, but in other cases, the men were not so fortunate:

> I left work feeling kind of down, and on my way home . . . I stopped in a bar where a friend of mine was bartending, and had two drinks there. And after that I left and I was pulled over by a squad car for weaving within my lane, and as a result of that an arrest was made and I spent the night in jail. That scared the hell out of me. (Scott)

Another man had been arrested for sexual solicitation:

> I got busted a year and a half ago in a park for what they call soliciting. It didn't turn out that's what they finally charged me

with. I had a good lawyer. That's what it was, to tell the truth. . . .
But that's the only time I've ever had any trouble with the law
because I was drinking. And I was really depressed at that time,
having problems with my wife, and I started drinking, and I went
to a park to pick somebody up, and I got busted. (Bruce)

There do not seem to have been long-range negative consequences
for the men in any of these instances. They spent a few hours in
jail, paid a fine, sometimes had their licenses suspended, but escaped
any general stigmatization. For example, Bruce's wife covered for
him by telling the family that he had been arrested for public intoxication.

Joining a Drinking Subculture

Over time, as the men entered the gay world, they continued
to use alcohol. This is not surprising, given the emphasis placed on
drinking as a social activity in the gay community. Entering the bar
scene slightly increased the alcohol consumption of a number of
men, while others stated that increases in drinking accompanied
their involvement in gay relationships outside of bar situations. For
example, Barry discovered the gay subculture when he was about
fifteen. He had been allowed to use alcohol at home, but when he
became involved with older gays and visited them in their homes,
he started to drink more.

Perceptions of Problems with Alcohol

I asked the men if there were ever any times when they had
consumed too much alcohol. All but six of them replied that this
had happened, and they gave a variety of reasons for why they had
felt this way. Three-fifths of them identified physical symptoms such
as feeling nauseous, passing out, having blackouts, becoming violent,
seeing double, staggering, losing track of time, being hung over,
and having been unable to drive as evidence of overindulgence.
Others cited emotional changes in themselves such as depression,
stress, or a "desperate" feeling as indicators of overconsumption of
alcohol. A few individuals identified party situations as the cause of

overindulgence in alcohol, while others realized later, with sudden insight, that they had been drinking too much.

One-quarter of the men who said they had sometimes had too much to drink identified this as a frequent, almost daily, situation. This is a much higher proportion than that found in studies of heterosexuals (Kraft, 1981).[5] As one might expect, this category included the recovering alcoholics. When asked what had been going on in their lives during this time, only two-thirds of the men were able to respond. Interestingly, 39% of them said that nothing unusual had been happening in their lives. Others identified a number of situations they felt had contributed to their excessive drinking: being disappointed or upset by a love or job situation (25%), participating in a party or celebration (13%), not coping well (10%), experiencing a change of situation (6%), being tired (3%), and being lonely (3%).

All but six men said they had at one time or another worried that they had been drinking too much as a lifestyle, rather than simply having overdone it on a particular occasion. However, most men were very passive about reducing their excessive drinking. While 44% of them did stop drinking temporarily, and another 17% reduced their drinking, only two men sought counseling. Another 36% of the men reported having done nothing about drinking too much, although one man said that he had "thought about it."

Three-fourths of the men reported having thought that they might have some problems with alcohol. The criteria they used included the amount and frequency of their alcohol use, their behavior while drinking, their motivations for drinking, their health problems and physical symptoms such as blackouts, and their family history of alcoholism.

> TOM: Have you ever thought you might have some problems with alcohol?

> GEORGE: Oh, definitely. . . because it has affected my health. It has affected my behavior. It has affected my emotional status.

> SULLY: Yeah. We've had a lot of alcoholics in my family, on both sides. . . . It killed my father's brother before I was born. I'm kind of a compulsive person and I'm prone to sudden mood changes. And people whom I know, who are recovered alcoholics, we've compared notes. I fit into everything except the drinking. So that's another reason why I watch it.

When asked more specifically whether they had experienced any alcohol-related problems, 72% of the men identified particular difficulties. This compares to 36% of the college students in Kraft's (1981) study, who identified drinking-related problem behavior during the past year. The largest proportion of these students (19%) identified only one problem. Problems reported by the students included drunk driving (30%), academic problems (22%), abusive/insulting behavior (16%), minor injuries (16%), sexual performance (15%), job problems (11%), property destruction (8%), and trouble with police (4%). The problems identified by the men I interviewed included fights and arguments (30%), physical ailments (26%), accidents (24%), arrests for public intoxication and driving under the influence (22%), lover problems (20%), loss of friends and family-related tensions (15%), sexual performance (13%), problems on the job (13%), ejection from bars (9%), school problems (7%), and having been robbed while intoxicated (4%).[6]

When the men were asked how others around them had responded to their drinking-related problem behavior, slightly fewer than half of them were able to identify specific responses. The others were not able to remember particular responses—probably because there were not any. Other people may have been unaware that anything was wrong because the men did not communicate their feelings to others. "Mostly, they didn't know about them," Todd said. Or, their behavior may have been perceived as normal within the expected bounds of gay sociability (Warren, 1974). Of the men who were able to respond to the question, only fifteen said they had received supportive feedback about their difficulties, which is not a strong indicator of support. Even more interesting is how the men felt about these responses. Only nine of the men who received support for their problems felt good about it. One man felt bad about the interest others had taken in his alcohol-related problems, and five others said that they had not cared what others had done. The respondents frequently reported that they were not interested in other peoples' responses to their problems; the one man who had received nonsupportive feedback said that he did not care, as did the men who said that they had not gotten any response from others.

> TOM: How did other people around you respond to the problems you had as a result of your drinking?
> VINNIE: They didn't want to deal with it. Nobody wanted to deal

with it. And now that I look back, I couldn't blame them, because I was just a cold sore, this ugly, ugly open wound, and wherever I went, everything seemed to turn to shit and I didn't know how to prevent it.

TOM: How did you feel about this lack of response?

VINNIE: Well, in the beginning, I was upset about it, and towards the end I became indifferent and it didn't matter to me. Besides, I didn't give a shit about them. So I realized that I couldn't give anything to them. I never did anything for them, so why should they do anything for me?

In general, the men did little about their concerns over alcohol use and related problems. Most merely decreased or discontinued drinking for short periods of time, while only a few men sought counseling or went into alcohol abuse programs. The lack of a serious effort to do something about their drinking problems is partly understandable, since as the men indicated in chapter 3, they had found few supports for sobriety within gay male community social life. Only eight men said that others were supportive of their attempts to deal with their drinking-related problems, and only five of these felt good about this feedback. Others, like Chuck, received only minimal support: "Yeah, it was more or less, 'I've been through it,' that kind of deal. I really didn't expect anything."

Abstinence and Relapse Cycles

Reasons for Abstention

Eighty percent of the men I interviewed reported having gone through periods when they did not drink. This includes both self-identified recovering alcoholics, and those who had labeled themselves as problem drinkers but were nevertheless still using alcohol. In most instances, these abstinent periods were relatively short, ranging from a few weeks to a few months. With a few exceptions, such as being on a Navy ship where alcohol was not easily accessible, most attempts at abstinence were voluntary. These periods of sobriety were consciously chosen and controlled, which is similar to what Wiseman (1979) found in a study of heterosexually married alcoholic men. Unlike those in Wiseman's sample, however, only a few men refrained from drinking for instrumental reasons such as fearing the loss of one's job, having college exams, visiting family, and the like.

> Tom: Have there ever been any periods in which you did not drink?
> Kevin: Well, short periods. But even when I was with my family for a couple of weeks about three or four years ago at the holidays—and they're pretty much teetotalers or were until the last few years—I still drank for relaxation, had a drink or two, a shot of bourbon or something in the evenings.

Health concerns were an important reason for abstention. Some men said that they had stopped because they were on a "health kick" (John), or because they were trying to lose weight (Joe and Gary), or because they wanted to "get into shape" and "clean out my system" (Alan). A few men mentioned having stomach ulcers or a general feeling of physical malaise; much more common were specific comments about having had hepatitis and therefore being unable to consume alcohol. This particular physical problem was quite prevalent.

Another significant reason some men gave for going through short periods of abstinence was to reassure themselves that they were not alcoholic. Their reasoning was that if they could voluntarily control their drinking, they could escape this self-definition. Abstinence was seen as a kind of experiment. In these cases the men were, in Wiseman's (1979) terms, self-consciously sober:

> There have been other times when I haven't been drinking where I pretty much did it to prove that I could do it. I wanted to make sure that I wasn't an alcoholic, and that I wasn't going to fall apart if I didn't drink . . . 'cause I definitely decided—I thought to myself—I have a substantial alcohol problem, and I'd better prove right now that it's just an environmental problem, and that it's not like I'm an alcoholic. (Gregory)

The relationships the men had with other people often precipitated periods of abstention. Ray (1961) found similar abstinence and relapse cycles among heroin addicts. The effect of others on the individual's decision to stop drinking was both direct and indirect. Significant others directly affected the man's periods of abstention

when they caused him to stop drinking to prove to them that he
could refrain from alcohol use:

> I think Ernie, several years ago, was worried about whether I was
> drinking too much, and so I laid off to show him I could. I don't
> remember even how long it was now. (Art)

> It's just these people I'm living with here . . . these people started
> giving me some shit about drinking, which I didn't feel was war-
> ranted because they don't drink at all, and they don't know or
> understand the drinking problem. . . . So I said, "Well, fine." You
> know, I didn't tell them this and they still don't know, but I did
> not drink for a week. (Jack)

Even more directly influential were situations in which another
person insisted that the respondent get help for his drinking problems. This had occurred for two men, who had both been heterosexually married. Their spouses asked them to go to AA or to addiction
hospitals. Additionally, physicians put them on Antabuse.

Indirect influences on an individual's abstinence were of two
kinds. Sometimes a man would look around him, observe other
people with drinking problems, and use them as negative role
models:

> I've had contact with somebody who's an alcoholic . . . and I'm
> really angry at some of the things that I see that she does that I
> know other alcoholics do also. Things like not taking responsibility
> for . . . the consequences of her behavior. And literally getting
> drunk every possible time and be[ing] really obnoxious. I've got so
> turned off by that, that at least for brief periods I've decided, shit,
> I'm not even going to touch that stuff. Look what it does to her.
> (Peter)

Another way that the attitudes and behavior of others indirectly
affected a man's abstinent periods was more subtle. A number of
men became involved in relationships with men who were light
drinkers or were abstinent. This de-emphasis on alcohol caused the
men to terminate their own drinking:

> I was around someone, or sort of having a relationship with a guy
> who was not very much of a partier and didn't drink very much

. . . so I made a lot of changes in myself. So I wasn't drinking any hard alcohol for a number of months. And I stopped drinking beer for a couple of months. (Ben)

Responses of Others to Abstention

The men reported having received little positive feedback from peers during their periods of abstinence. When they were asked about the responses of others to these times, ten of them (27% of those having gone through such periods) said that the feedback they had received was positive. However, six of these men reported that those positive responses were not from the gay community but from their wives or from fellow members of AA. All but three of the ten men reporting at least some positive responses said that their attempts at sobriety were also viewed negatively or ignored within the gay community. The reactions from friends were normally negative, mixed, or, most often, noncommittal.

> TOM: How did other people around you respond to your stopping drinking?
>
> BEN: They thought I was a little nuts. Like, "What's going on?" You know, "Do you think you're becoming an alcoholic or something?" Or, "What's the big change?" "How come? Don't you like to party any more?"
>
> BRUCE: Very matter-of-factly, as if it didn't make a damn [bit of difference], which annoyed me. I figured I had accomplished a tremendous amount, and I wasn't getting any congratulations. I wasn't getting any, "Well, Jeez, it's nice to see you sober," or "We're really glad that you were able to do it." No, you know, plaudits, no good hands, nothing. I found that they accepted the fact that I quit drinking, and "Let's go on to the next thing." Then I felt like, if I did something this wonderful, and this was such a major achievement for me, why doesn't somebody say something to me? And it was a struggle to stay sober.

Returning to Alcohol Use

Bruce's comments illustrate a point made by Ray (1961):

During the early phases of an episode of abstinence the abstainer enters various situations with quite definite expectations concerning how he should be defined and treated. He indicates his desire for ratification of his new status in many ways, and finds it socially difficult when he sees in the conduct of others toward him a reference to his old identity as an addict. (p. 138)

Ray indicates that relapse can result from the failure of others to validate the individual's new self-perception. Ultimately, "relapse is a function of the kind of object ex-addicts make of themselves in the situations they face" (p. 138). Similar perceptions were held by some of the abstinent gay drinkers in this study. It matters little whether one's attempts at—and claims of—sobriety are questioned, dismissed, or ignored. The resultant feelings of rejection are the same.

The social linkages of alcohol use with the gay community were important factors that caused a number of men to resume drinking. They indicated that drinking was necessary for social acceptance, that alcohol was part of their lifestyle, or that they were offered alcohol by friends.

TOM: Why did you begin drinking again?

PAUL: Because I got out of school and then I started meeting people who were more into . . . that type of social life. And, I did begin to feel kind of lonely after I left school and I didn't have the same contacts that I did [before].

RICHARD: Just spontaneously I decided I wasn't going to drink. . . . I didn't do it for seven weeks. And then a friend from out of town, an old lover came in from out of town, and again it was a social situation and I started.

For others, having stopped drinking was defined as an experiment, so that after they had satisfied themselves (and sometimes others) that they could refrain from alcohol use, they saw no reason to continue to abstain. Over one-third of the men said that they had resumed drinking for no particular reason. Their responses, how-ever, indicate that drinking had become very much a part of their lifestyles.

TOM: And why did you resume drinking?

ART: Because I enjoy drinking. I like the taste of beer and I like the taste of bourbon, and so I drink it.

PATRICK: Choice. No particular event.

NORMAN: I just decided to drink one day, I don't know [why].

Current Alcohol Use

The assertion made in chapter 3 that drinking is a social activity for most gay men was verified when they were asked to explain why they currently drank. One-fourth of the men said that their primary motivation for using alcohol was to express sociability. A similar proportion said that they used alcohol to feel at ease in social situations. They claimed that drinking helped them relax, lose their inhibitions, and reduce their anxiety in meeting potential sexual partners: "I felt more creative sexually, of course less inhibited. I felt that I could be more aggressive sexually and whatever, and more desirable and all of that" (Joel). Somewhat fewer men noted that alcohol consumption was expected behavior in the bars. Thus, they directly tied their drinking to social expectations:

> Now, basically, I think that the reason I drink is that it is the thing to do when you're standing around a bar. It lubricates the scene and makes you feel good. (Daniel)

> You know, if you are in the bar, I thought you had to be drinking. (Todd)

Some men identified alcohol use as part of their lifestyle, and indicated that most of their drinking took place in their home: "Usually, on the average, I'll say we probably just drink out of habit more than anything. You know, it's just standard to come home, change clothes, and make a drink, without a second thought" (Frank).

In contrast with the men cited above who drank as part of social expectations that were integrated into a particular lifestyle, others focused on the physical properties of alcohol and used it instrumentally to achieve a particular effect. So, for example, some men told me that they drank primarily because they enjoyed the taste of alcohol or the feelings it gave them. Others used alcohol to cope with stress and to counter depression:

> I started drinking really heavily—and I say that's drinking versus just social drinking—because I was gay, because I couldn't handle my marriage, couldn't handle the jobs I was in. . . . Usually it was in a depressed situation. When I become depressed, I drink. And I drink heavily. Actually, the happier I am, the less I drink. And it's more an emotional basis than anything else. (Bruce)

One-third of the men said that their reasons for drinking were relatively stable and did not vary much with the situation. Others, however, were able to identify specific conditions that affected their motivation to drink. For instance, almost one-fifth said that social environments, especially those requiring sociability, such as parties and other celebrations, would cause them to drink to fit in. Other men said that they would be more motivated to drink to relieve stressful situations on the job, to escape domestic problems, to cool off on a hot day, to close business deals, or to use as a catalyst for a night out. Some men stated that their reasons for using alcohol varied with the situation, but they could not give specific examples.

Alcohol use was generally viewed very positively by the men in this study. When they were asked how they usually felt when they were drinking, almost half of the men said that they generally felt good, happy, and relaxed. Others were more specific, indicating that alcohol made them feel "hyper," (i.e., charged with energy in a positive sense), less inhibited, and less concerned with the opinions of others.

Not all men saw alcohol use as uniformly positive. For example, five of those individuals who claimed to feel good initially when drinking also said that as they continued ingesting alcohol over the evening, they became progressively more and more depressed or hostile.

> Tom: How do you usually feel when you've been drinking?
> Chuck: That depends on what's going on in my life at the time. Usually, right at first, my first couple of drinks I'll just feel real mellow and relaxed and then I'll get three or four and start to get real crazy. But then again it depends. It can be reversed—

I'll feel good the first couple of drinks and then I'll go downhill
and I'll get real depressed.

A few respondents simply said that alcohol had no positive features
for them and inevitably made them feel anxious, hostile, or depressed. Other men responded to the question in terms of physical
symptoms rather than referring to social behavior. They indicated
that alcohol made them sleepy, ill, caused their ears to burn, and
so on. Only one man, who was a very light drinker, said that alcohol
had no effect upon him.

Alcohol is an important element in the lives of many gay men.
Although they generally do not begin drinking in the gay world,
the social aspects of that subculture influence their patterns of alcohol
use. By utilizing the notion of career, it has been possible to organize
and examine drinking behavior as a process that is continually affected by social definitions and the responses of others.

The men in this study began to use alcohol at about the same
age as most heterosexuals. At that time, their behavior was really
no different from that of most young people. Like their heterosexual
peers, they were not concerned about developing drinking problems; they either enjoyed alcohol or did not give it much thought.
Almost all of them began drinking prior to coming out. Once they
did come out, however, their alcohol use began to increase.

Almost all of the men reported that they occasionally had too
much to drink, but this probably does not differentiate them from
most people who imbibe. What is interesting is that more than one-
fifth of the gay men reported having overdone it several times a
week. This is a much higher proportion than that found in studies
of college students. Even more striking is that 87% of the men I
spoke with said they had worried they were drinking too much as
a lifestyle, and that three-quarters of all my respondents thought
they might have some problems with alcohol. Seventy-two percent
of the men described problems that were the result of alcohol use,
which is twice the proportion of college students who identify drinking-related problems. The gay men were much more likely to report
interpersonal problems (fights, arguments, and conflicts with family,
lovers, and friends) than were the college students. They were more
than five times as likely to indicate having had trouble with the
police. However, problems with sexual performance and jobs were

noted by similar percentages in each group, as were accidents (gays) and injuries and property destruction (college students).

One striking finding that emerges in this chapter is that social supports for drinking-related problems and an individual's attempts to deal with them were usually lacking. Failure of others to encourage an individual's development of a nonuser identity is, of course, not confined to the gay world. Wiseman (1970), for example, has shown that the absence of these supports contributes importantly to the failure of men who return to skid row after being discharged from rehabilitation programs. In fact, the indifference of others to a person's attempts at sobriety is probably a general feature of our society. What seems to be a special problem for gays is that their choice of alternative groups is more restricted than it is for nongays. Gays, therefore, have the unappealing choice of either abstaining from alcohol and social interaction, or continuing to drink and participating in an alcohol-centered subculture and taking their chances with alcohol. The dilemma of gays with drinking problems is illustrated by the finding that while 80% of the men in this study had gone through abstinent periods, almost all of them had returned to alcohol use. They usually began drinking again because alcohol was an integral part of their lifestyles and social networks. While there are some nondrinking subcultures of gay men apart from organizations such as Alcoholics Together and Gay AA, many men do not know how to seek them out. A number of lighter drinkers in this study, however, have been successful in finding alternative social outlets to the bars.

Frequency and Amount of Drinking

I classified the drinkers I interviewed based on the amount of alcohol they usually consumed over a given period of time (see table 4). While there is a wide range of drinking represented, most drinkers fall within the moderately heavy to heavy categories. However, as I cautioned in chapter 2, this finding may not represent the distribution of alcohol use within the gay male subculture, but may simply be a function of how the data were collected.

Drinking was an everyday event for many of the men and a frequent activity for others. Fifteen men (33%) used alcohol every day, five men (11%) drank five to six times a week, nine men (20%) used alcohol three to four times a week, and eight men (17%) drank once or twice a week. Three men (6%) drank less than once a week.[7]

Table 4. *Classification of Drinkers in the Study*

Category	n^a	%
Abstainers (all recovering alcoholics)	6	13
Infrequent drinkers	1	2
Light drinkers	2	4
Moderate drinkers	7	15
Moderately heavy drinkers	22	48
Heavy drinkers	8	18
TOTAL	46	100

[a]These classifications were made following Engs's (1977) modification of the Straus and Bacon (1953) Quantity-Frequency Index, which takes into account the absolute alcohol content of various drinks, as well as the number of drinks used over a given period of time.

In contrast, Kraft (1981) reported that only 12% of his respondents used alcohol as frequently as three to four times a week, 27% drank once or twice a week, and 16% drank less than once a week. He characterized only 7% of his sample as heavy drinkers, 46% as moderate drinkers, 40% as light users of alcohol, and 7% as abstainers.

A number of men indicated that alcohol use had become well integrated into their lifestyles:

> Almost every day I drink some beer in the evenings. And two or three times a week I guess I would be what you call drunk. Two or three times a week, maybe more, depending upon the period in my life, what else is going on. But that's regular. Sometimes I go through periods where I don't drink for a week or so, but that's about it. That's regular. It's just part of my life. It's always there. (Kevin)

The amount of alcohol consumed during a drinking episode varied, but not widely, since most men had between two and five drinks at a given time. The men tended to regulate their drinking depending on a variety of factors: whether they were at home, at a party, or in a bar, whether they were alone or with others, whether they were drinking during the week or on a weekend, and whether or not they intended to make a sexual contact. Maintaining control over their drinking was an important concern for many of the men and was often spontaneously mentioned by them during the course of an interview.

7. Infrequent, Light, and Moderate Drinkers

Among the twenty-five men I interviewed who have no problems with their drinking is a particularly interesting subgroup of infrequent, light, and moderate drinkers, who integrate alcohol use into their everyday lives and social relationships and function well. In contrast to the other men, who are moderately heavy consumers of alcohol, these nine individuals do not place great importance on drinking. While they only constitute one-fifth of my respondents, there is a possibility that they are underrepresented. Larry, who is a light drinker, commented, "I know there are an awful lot of [gay people] who don't drink any more than I do. They drink only when it's kind of forced upon them socially, just to be sociable, and they will drink the one glass of wine or a few, and maybe never drink again until they're in a similar situation." By examining Larry's drinking history and those of the other men who are lighter drinkers, it is possible to gain some insight into the factors related to variations in alcohol use in the gay male community. The drinking histories of these men and their social relationships are of special interest as they affect alcohol use.

Early Drinking Experiences

Lighter drinkers tended to have begun using alcohol at later ages than men who were more avid consumers of alcohol. Almost

94

all of them were at least twenty-one years old, and some were considerably older, when they started drinking. Clifford, for example, who is an infrequent drinker, began going to gay bars at the age of twenty-one, but he did not start drinking until he was twenty-four. When he first began attending bars, Clifford would order soft drinks. "I did not drink alcohol when I went to a bar until recently," he said, "when I felt I'd built up a tolerance and could take one or two drinks." His coming out occurred prior to entering the bar scene, by going to "the social center for gays." He uses alcohol "maybe twice a year" and orders nonalcoholic beverages such as 7-up, ginger ale, or sparkling water during his bar visits. He rarely uses alcohol because of how it makes him feel.

> CLIFFORD: When I start feeling it, the alcohol taking effect, I get very uncomfortable. I feel I am losing control.
> TOM: Does that bother you in any way?
> CLIFFORD: Yes. It bothers me very much. That's why I drink very little or not at all.

Art had gone to nongay bars sometime after the age of twenty-one, but he began drinking fairly frequently between the ages of thirty and thirty-five. He was in his early fifties before he became aware of a gay community, and he came out and began drinking in gay bars at the age of fifty-eight. He is still not "out" to everyone he knows. Larry also came out late. He first went to a gay bar at the age of sixty-five. Like Art, he said, "I'm really not thoroughly out of the closet. Only with my gay friends." Larry considers himself to be homosexual, rather than gay, because he does not participate very much in a gay lifestyle. The reasons why both Art and Larry deferred their coming out are similar. The first of these is the stigma that was placed on homosexuality during the time they were young men. Art related, "In those earlier years, I tended to be a lone wolf, because I knew I was different and I didn't have friends who knew it, in general. And so, I stayed pretty much alone. I just could not go out and make a scene of going to pick up girls." Larry told me, "You must remember, [for] a larger portion of my share . . . of life, the word *gay* hadn't even been invented, and every homosexually inclined individual was in the closet. They had to be, in most instances, at least. And I was in a position where I definitely had to be." A second reason is that both men took on the responsibility of caring for elderly relatives, which restricted them from going out and socializing in the gay world until after these people had died.

Ernie is Art's lover. He occasionally drank with his family and a neighbor when he was in his early teens, but he began using alcohol more consistently when he left home at the age of eighteen. At that time, he met Art and moved in with him. Until he was twenty-one, his drinking was confined to their home or to those of friends, for dinners and at parties. His infrequent visits to gay bars, once or twice a month, began when he was legally able to enter them.

Carl is twenty-seven years old. He began drinking at the age of twenty-four, which was the first time he went to any kind of bar. Raised in a fundamentalist family, he went to a religious college, which accounts for his later use of alcohol. His first drinking experience was with heterosexual friends in a "straight" bar. Carl feels that he has a high susceptibility to alcohol, a perception shared with other moderate and light drinkers.

> TOM: About how many drinks do you usually have when you're drinking?
>
> PAUL: Two. I have a very low immunity to alcohol . . . three will make me sick. I have a weak stomach.

Like Carl, many of the other light or moderate drinkers began using alcohol before they ever entered the gay world. But unlike him, some of them had periods during which they drank quite heavily. Paul, for example, started drinking with heterosexual friends. He had always been fearful of drugs and alcohol, because his mother had died of alcoholism and his father was an alcoholic. He began drinking because of peer pressure and drank mostly at parties. He says that at first, he got no pleasure from drinking and had "a lot of guilt" over it. When friends plied him with beer, Paul would sneak into the bathroom and pour it into the toilet: "I was drinking about one beer at the most," he said. "I felt that for me, at that time, I felt I hated beer. I hated the taste of it. I couldn't stand it." At the age of twenty-two he was drafted, and he began drinking what he considers to be "quite a lot," because he felt under pressure by his commanding officer. Eventually, he developed an ulcer.

Michael first began drinking at the age of twenty-two. His best friend at work introduced him to a woman whom he started dating, and he married her shortly thereafter:

> It wasn't until my ex-wife and I got together that I drank socially. In fact, I think I could be what you call . . . a prude and a puritan. And I really looked down on it. Both of my parents were alcoholics and my grandparents were teetotalers, and my grandparents always looked down on my parents for it. I was brought up in a fundamentalist church . . . and it was something that was taboo and sinful and that I simply . . . wouldn't have done.

At first, Michael was fearful about drinking. Soon, however, "I got drunk for the first time and that was really great. I had never been so uninhibited and happy . . . in my whole life. And so, alcohol was suddenly great." During his short-lived marriage, Michael was consuming three to four drinks daily. Within a month of his marital breakup, Michael began going to gay bars and having sexual encounters with other men. He says, "I got drunk quite a few times in those days, and I think my average was to consume about a pitcher, a pitcher-and-a-half when it wasn't a worknight, because I was in there every day of the week."

Tim began drinking at about the age of twenty, when he was a college student. This was roughly during the same period that he decided that he was gay. At that time, he said, "I thought [alcohol] was great. I thought it was a great discovery." Within the year, he began going to gay bars and drinking heavily, from three to six drinks during his bar visits, which at one point were nightly occurrences. Along with alcohol, he smoked marijuana and took other drugs.

Peter drank heavily when he first came out to the gay bars at the age of twenty-seven or twenty-eight. He was doing this two or three times a week, and consuming "probably four or five drinks" of scotch or bourbon. "At the beginning," he remembers, "I always drank a lot, to the point where it was questionable whether I could drive. . . . It was consistent. I never left a bar any way but almost drunk. It was an absolute given." He attributes his heavy drinking to being nervous about being in the bar setting. His first experience with alcohol came earlier, however, when he was in graduate school. At that time he would go to what he called a "hippie bar" and drink "lots of beer." Between this period and his coming out, Peter says that he did not drink much at bars. His alcohol consumption was limited to dinners.

For these light and moderate drinkers as a group, drinking usually occurred prior to coming out and often with nongay friends. While some of them deferred drinking until after beginning to visit gay bars, others drank heavily at that time or even before they had entered the gay world. They attributed their heavy drinking to peer pressure, job-related tension, anxiety over being in a gay bar, the need for getting over sexual inhibitions, and the overindulgence that sometimes accompanies new experiences.

Current Drinking Practices

In contrast to their earlier use of alcohol, all of these men are now much lighter drinkers. Paul no longer drinks the way he once did. Usually, he uses alcohol about once a week. Even when he is in a social situation, he says he will tell his friends, "I won't drink, you go ahead and drink." The major exception to his general avoidance of alcohol is when he is under stress. During those times Paul says that he will drink.

Michael drinks about once a week, "mostly wine and once in a while a liqueur." He generally has two or three drinks, most often with dinner. Michael says, "I don't think it's too fashionable to drink anymore. Drinking to go along with the crowd doesn't make much sense any longer."

Tim drinks twice a month. He prefers champagne and wine and has two, "maybe three," drinks at a time. He usually drinks at home or at someone else's home. "Usually I won't even drink at parties these days," he told me. "It's almost to the point where it's hard for me to imagine that I used to drink as much as I did. You know, there's been times that I've sat and I've looked back at what I used to do and just not been able to imagine that I actually did it." He noted, "I've lost my ease of drinking a lot. I'm not used to it, anymore. If I have a couple of drinks, I won't necessarily feel great, I may feel sick. I never used to feel sick when I drank."

Peter reports drinking "maybe a couple of times a week." Until about two weeks before I interviewed him, his drinking had been confined to wine with dinner. Then he discovered the Sultan, the piano bar located close to his office. He began going there and participating in singing with the other patrons. Peter enjoys the social recognition he has been getting from others at the bar: "It's social, primarily, and also recognition in terms of the singing. People know my name now; I get greeted when I walk in and, you know, 'When are you gonna sing? How come you are late tonight? We were wondering when you were going to get here'." Peter's drinking has begun to increase since he began visiting the Sultan. He is now drinking two or three Black Russians before he sings, and that bothers him. "The fact that I feel the need to have . . . a couple of drinks before I can do it bugs the shit out of me," he told me.

To understand how these changes in alcohol consumption have occurred, and how a number of the men have become light or moderate drinkers, it is necessary to examine their social relationships and lifestyles, which are related both to alcohol consumption and to the settings in which they drink.

Social Relationships and Drinking

Decreases in the drinking of formerly heavier drinkers can be explained by the relationships they have developed with other people. One of the important differences between these lighter drinkers and many of the other men I talked to is that over time, they have cultivated friendships in a variety of settings outside the gay bars. These relationships allow them to participate in social activities with other gay people in situations that are not alcohol-related. They are also more likely to meet other gay men who are not bar habitués or heavy drinkers. Larry has a group of gay friends, most of whom he met through the Metropolitan Community Church. None of these people are heavy drinkers.

> Tom: Do your friends drink alcoholic beverages?
> Larry: Most of them do more than I. But now, my closer friends, they certainly do not overindulge. They drink more than I, but not to excess.

Michael is representative of these lighter drinkers. He has expanded his social contacts since his earlier participation in the gay world. He has heterosexual friends and several groups of gay friends. "Some of my gay friends know each other, others of them don't," he said. "It's not really [due] to my segregating them as much as it's different reasons I know them and different reasons they are friends. My most intimate friends know one another." Michael is very active in a number of gay organizations and has made friends through the Gay Center, the gay businessmen's association, the Metropolitan Community Church, Lutherans Concerned, Dignity, and Integrity (an organization for gay Episcopalians). While he occasionally goes to the bars with friends, most of his socializing takes place in other situations. He noted, "I have a lot of social involvement and I don't really need the bars." Instead, his social life revolves around getting together with friends for dinner and social visits at home. Sometimes he'll have wine on these occasions, which are not, however, as commonplace as nonalcoholic evenings are. "I think the majority of my friends don't drink," Michael observed. He does not serve alcohol to dinner guests unless "it's someone who drinks alcohol and likes their alcohol—then, I will do it. If it's someone who drinks about the pace I do, I don't serve any alcohol at all." In contrast to the people with whom he originally drank, Michael says that his current friends are happy, well adjusted, and not "running from themselves." His earlier gay drinking companions "really weren't too happy or too well adjusted to their gayness or to life in general or to both." Like his friends, Michael is happy with himself and with his life. On being homosexual, he says, "It's the greatest thing that ever happened to me." The other lighter drinkers have similar feelings about their sexual orientation, themselves, and their lives. They accept themselves and enjoy their lives.

The current relationships and drinking patterns of the other infrequent, light, and moderate drinkers are similar to those of Michael and Larry. Their friends, who are also light or moderate drinkers, are made through participation in the Metropolitan Community Church, the Gay Center, and other gay organizations. In general, they are actively involved in these gay institutions. Their drinking tends to be confined to dinner parties and other social events such as those sponsored by gay organizations, and on these occasions they drink lightly or not at all. They are more interested in socializing than in getting intoxicated. As Ernie puts it, "At parties and the like, I tend to drink just to be sort of sociable and that type of thing, you know. But as far as drinking itself, it's always been just for a pleasurable experience."

Peter's situation is the exception because he has few social relationships outside the Sultan. This is why the recognition he is getting in the bar is so important to him, and also why his drinking has begun to accelerate. When I asked him, "Do you have a group of gay friends?" he replied, "No. I don't have anybody that I would consider a close friend who's gay." He went on to tell me, "I've never had a network of gay friends. At most, I've known and had some contact with maybe two or three. There are a group of people [at the Gay Center] with whom I have a fair amount of contact and with whom I work, and we're in a sense, sort of friends, or at least some of us are." Peter noted that he doesn't "get invited to parties that much" or to other people's homes very frequently.

Lighter Drinkers and the Bars

One of the striking differences between these men and the others I have interviewed is that they are infrequent bar visitors. Carl, for example, attends the bars only sporadically, once a month or so, "kind of few and far between," he said. "I don't really enjoy going to gay bars," he told me, "because they're kind of boring; all there is to do is drink. And that's why I tend to avoid them." Larry says that he rarely goes out to bars, "particularly since I don't really come to drink—I'd wonder what to do."

Tim said, "I don't go to bars very much, and when I do, I usually don't buy drinks unless it's kind of pushed on me. And then, I usually don't drink." Michael does go out to bars, but only when invited by friends. He goes to dance, and he drinks coffee or 7-up, rather than alcohol. After getting involved with the Metropolitan Community Church and other gay organizations, he "started getting invited to more private parties . . . to where I had social friends I was seeing regularly at home and at parties in homes, rather than at the bars. And so, it was sort of a bits-and-pieces type of getting out of what I'd call the bar syndrome."

Although Clifford had visited gay bars almost every weekend in the past, he no longer does so. He said, "Now, I don't find the need to go out to a bar. . . . I don't meet the type of people in bars that I am interested in making friends with. . . . To be totally honest, the bar scene is not my thing." Instead, he has a small group of friends whom he has met at the Metropolitan Community Church or the Gay Center. Like him, they are light drinkers who do not spend time in the bar.

In sum, these infrequent, light, and moderate drinkers spend

little time in the bars and are not involved in bar culture. They
socialize with others whom they meet at the Metropolitan Community Church, the Gay Center, and other organizations. Their lives
revolve around these voluntary organizations and the friendships
they make in them. They have guests over for dinner, and they
attend dinners and private parties. Since their friends tend to be
lighter drinkers, these occasions are frequently alcohol-free. These
men do not isolate themselves in the gay world; they often have
close friendships with nongay friends with whom they also spend
time. They have positive attitudes toward being gay; they like themselves and are generally satisfied with their lives.

8. Problem Drinkers

In chapter 6, I examined a variety of issues involved in the drinking behavior of the men in this study. Here I turn to a more detailed examination of the drinking careers of the men who have experienced more consistent difficulty with alcohol. While many men I interviewed use alcohol, not all of them defined themselves as drinkers in the sense that alcohol is central to their perception of who they are.[1] Fewer still come to see themselves as problem drinkers. To conceptualize oneself in either way requires making a connection between what one does and what one is, as symbolized by one's behavior (Matza, 1969). The questions to be examined in this chapter are, How do men come to define themselves as problem drinkers?, and, Under what conditions do they decide to do something about their problems?

The problem drinkers in this study fall into three general categories: (1) researcher-identified problem drinkers, (2) self-identified alcoholics who are still drinking, and (3) self-identified recovering alcoholics. Criteria used to define the men in the first category as problem drinkers include their classification as heavy or moderately heavy drinkers on the modified Quantity-Frequency Index, combined with their own reports of physical problems with alcohol such as blackouts; medical illnesses affecting the function of their livers and gastrointestinal and cardiovascular systems; alcohol-related legal problems such as arrests for driving while intoxicated or public intoxication; social and interpersonal problems including fights, ejection from bars, lover and friendship schisms; and accidents. All eleven men I classified as problem drinkers had difficulties in several of these areas. In developing this typology, I gave less weight to the amount of alcohol consumed than to these other criteria. Following

103

Goode (1989), I do not see heavy drinking and problem drinking as necessarily synonymous. "The notion of a problem drinker is based on *how people see what happens to the drinker's life* [Goode's italics]. . . . Being considered a problem drinker," Goode writes, "is a result of a combination of drinking and how this behavior is reacted to by others as well as the drinker. . . . A problem drinker, then, is quite simply someone who gets into trouble—directly or indirectly—because of consuming alcohol" (p. 130).

Four respondents fell into the second category. They described themselves as alcoholics during their interviews, and are currently still drinking. Six other men made up the third category of problem drinkers. They are self-avowed recovering alcoholics, most of whom are active participants in AA. At the time of their interviews, they had been abstinent for periods ranging from two months to five years.[2]

The category of researcher-identified problem drinker appears at first glance to violate the consistency of my typology construction, since it includes "objective" criteria as opposed to the subjective interpretations used to classify men as either self-identified still drinking alcoholics or self-identified recovering alcoholics. A related question is whether such categories are real or analytical. All of these categories have a social or phenomenological reality in the sense that they reflect people's perceptions of their own and others' drinking. Although the men I categorized as researcher-identified problem drinkers denied heavy, problematic involvement with alcohol, all of them were perceived by others as having such difficulties. Chapter 3, for example, described how many of P. J.'s friends had become very concerned about his drinking and related behavior. John, who reported that friends had defined his own drinking as alcoholic (an allegation that he denied), nevertheless had no reservations about labeling his roommate, Patrick, another researcher-identified problem drinker, as an alcoholic:

> My roommate is an alcoholic, with no question about it. . . . I don't think of myself in terms of being an alcoholic because I've never felt a compulsion from the alcohol, merely a compulsion from the situations. . . . Now my roommate on the other hand, cannot stop drinking. I can go out and have one drink and be perfectly happy not to drink anymore. But he can't. If he drinks one, if he drinks

one vodka, it's vodka for the rest of the evening. . . . I worry about him. He's gotten a couple of 5-0-2s and he beat the last one. But the drinking can affect his life negatively.

The difference between the men described in this chapter and the nonproblem drinkers included in the discussion of drinking careers is that the problem drinkers use alcohol a good deal more, and they get into trouble because of their drinking. The following descriptions highlight similarities and differences among the three categories of problem drinkers.

Researcher-identified Problem Drinkers

These men's behavior revolves around their alcohol use, and other aspects of their lives become organized in terms of drinking as well. At this point, they have assumed the role of drinker, and they often engage in secondary deviance in support of this role (Lemert, 1951). These men, who had been drinking for a median time of eleven years (with a range of three to eighteen years), used alcohol at least four or five times a week, and half of them drank daily. The men tended to drink heavily: half of them consumed at least ten drinks during a drinking episode, three others said they would have six to eight drinks, and two of them usually consumed about four drinks. Alan, who worked in a bar, was typical of those who drank every day. He combined daily drinking with a high consumption during the course of an evening: "I usually drink a lot," he said. "I guzzle. So, twelve drinks a night, plus shots."

In addition to the frequency and quantity of alcohol they consume, there is other evidence that these men are flirting with alcoholism. For example, all of them drink alone and use alcohol when they are under stress or depressed, behavior which, according to Jellinek (1960, 1962), is characteristic of prealcoholics.[3]

TOM: Do you ever drink alone?

RICHARD: Yes. [When I'm bored or frustrated.] Maybe something at work is not going the way I want it—I'm being pressured by the boss. And I come home and there's a period I'm alone there in that house, I'll take a couple of drinks before dinner. Those are the times I tend to do it.

JOHN: I tend to drink more when I am depressed. And, if I am out some place and don't really want to be there, I'll drink more.

Additionally, the motives and interests of a number of these men have become increasingly centered around alcohol. A night out or a party become defined in terms of their potential for drinking, rather than as social events. Jellinek (1962) points out that "when [the individual] prepares to go to a social gathering his first thought is whether there will be sufficient alcohol for his requirements, and he has several drinks in anticipation of a possible shortage" (p. 362). This was true for the researcher-identified problem drinkers. These men frequently drink as a prelude to going to the bar, in order to make sure that they will have enough alcohol: "And if I go out dancing, I'll start before I go out and then when I get there [I'll continue drinking]. It's a little bit cheaper when you go out. It makes it fun going over there" (Jeffrey). Another way to be certain that enough alcohol will be available is to bring it along.

TOM: [Do you drink at] other people's homes? Friends' homes? Parties?
SCOTT: Yes, I usually drink there. In fact, I will—if wine, for instance, is not likely to be, oh, accompany dinner, I usually can be counted on to bring some.

The men have also begun to experience difficulties as a direct result of their drinking. They have developed health and financial problems, had physical confrontations while drinking, lost friends and had lover problems, been thrown out of bars, had problems on the job, been arrested for driving while intoxicated, had other run-ins with police when drinking, and gotten into automobile accidents. A number of them report having become loud, argumentative, and obnoxious during a drinking episode.

TOM: Have you ever had any fights when you've been drinking?
P. J.: Oh, yeah. I get loud and obnoxious and belligerent . . . and we've had some pretty knock-down-drag-out fights.

Other men experience what seem to be blackouts and sometimes do not remember what they have done.

TOM: Are there times when you feel that you've had too much to drink?

GEORGE: Oh, yes.

TOM: What are those times like?

GEORGE: You mean such things as I can't remember what happened or what I did or said?

TOM: Has that happened?

GEORGE: Has it happened? Yes.

Despite the dramatic nature of some of their drinking-related experiences, and even though all of them say that they sometimes have had too much to drink or even that they worried that they have been drinking too much, the men are reluctant to label themselves as alcoholics. P. J., for instance, says, "I probably drink more than I should on occasion, but I would not say I'm an alcoholic." He has developed a series of rationalizations to account for his drunken driving arrests, occasional conflicts when drinking, and tendency to overdo his drinking at parties, situations within which any "drinker" may sometimes find him- or herself. Gays, of course, are not alone in doing this. Rudy (1986) notes that "when A.A. members received queries about their drinking from family and friends as well as from formal agents of social control, their typical response was denial. Mideastern City A.A. members try to negotiate other explanations for their drinking behavior" (p. 100). Warren (1974) observes that gay men make a distinction between normal drunkenness and alcoholism (pp. 58–59). P. J.'s comments reflect such an attempt to make his drinking seem normal:

> I think there are a lot of people today who are being told they're alcoholics when they're not really alcoholics. . . . I think all of us probably go through periods in our life when, if we are drinkers, we probably drink a little bit heavier, and because you drink heavier it's possible to get a DWI or something like that, or maybe get in more arguments with a spouse or loved one, or a lover, than normal. But I don't necessarily think that makes you an alcoholic. I think it's a period of time when you're probably not in tune with yourself.

Responding to criticisms he had encountered after having attended a party and become "super drunk" as the result of having finished "about a quart and a half of gin and bourbon all by myself," he said, "But as far as I was concerned, it was a bit of overreacting."

In resisting the alcoholic label, other men were more sophisticated than P. J. They equated alcoholism with lack of control over
their drinking. As long as they were drinking because they wanted
to and could cut back on their drinking, they did not feel the necessity
of labeling themselves as alcoholics. John, for instance, has thought
that he might have some problems with alcohol. "Sure," he said, "I
think anybody who drinks as consistently as I do, and who wants it
[may have problems]." Yet he has never done anything about his
difficulties with alcohol because "I tend to equate alcoholism with
loss of control, and I don't like the idea of not being in control. My
attitude about my drinking is that I drink when I want to drink, and
if I didn't want to drink, I wouldn't do it." John's sentiments were
echoed by Jack, who said, "I'm becoming more alcohol-aware, realizing that I have a great potential of becoming a superalcoholic, and
I don't want that. And then again, I don't want to stop drinking,
either. It's something I'm going to have to control."

Some of these men came even closer to admitting that they
had a drinking problem, without coming out and actually labeling
themselves as alcoholics. For instance, in discussing his past behavior, Patrick said, "Probably I was about as close to being an alcoholic
as you can get." He had experienced the loss of friends, fights,
ejection from bars, and two drunken driving arrests, the most recent
of which had occurred just a few weeks prior to his interview. Asked
if he had ever thought that he might have some problems with
alcohol, he replied affirmatively. "How many people need twelve
doubles?" he asked me.

Self-identified Alcoholics Who Are Still Drinking

The careers of the self-identified alcoholics who are still drinking differed from those of the researcher-identified problem drinkers, primarily in the conceptualization of self as problem drinker.
These men have begun to label their drinking, and consequently
themselves, as alcoholic. Such a redefinition is not easily done because it involves bridging the gap between behavior (doing) and the
implications of this behavior for one's self-identity (being) (Matza,
1969), with consequent changes in one's moral career (Goffman,
1959). Even when the individual has experienced numerous serious
problems as a result of his drinking, he may still resist labeling

himself as an alcoholic. For example, Bruce reported that he had been arrested for soliciting while under the influence of alcohol and that he had attempted suicide three times when he was drunk. At one point, he got violent when he was drinking and beat up his son-in-law. Yet he did not think he had a drinking problem, primarily because he felt he could control his drinking. "At first I really didn't realize that I was drinking that heavy," he said. "I just started buying it and drinking it, feeling that I could handle anything that I wanted to drink—I could handle it, it was no problem. And it just got out of control rapidly." Finally, however, he had to face the implications of his alcohol use:

> I've known I've had a problem with alcohol for a long time. Long time. But you can't ever be honest with anyone except maybe another alcoholic who admits he's an alcoholic. Maybe that's why AA has done so well for so many people—they're all there under the same circumstances. But it was hard for me to realize that I was an alcoholic. I wouldn't admit that to myself probably for a good year or two after I was really drinking heavy. And I fought it and fought it and fought it, and when I finally said, "Okay, you're an alcoholic," I felt better about myself because I figured, "Dumb ass, you've answered your own question about what's going on in your life, and if you know you're an alcoholic, then you can start dealing with that." (Bruce)

In general, people who acquire the self-label of alcoholic realize that their behavior is extreme. When their drinking occurs within a group of similarly hard-drinking friends, however, it is more difficult for people to recognize extreme behavior. To a large extent, our self-perceptions depend on the social context—the definitions others bring to the situations in which we participate. Thus, if everyone else is behaving in a certain way, this behavior is never critically examined by anyone and is seen as normal. Nevertheless, some individuals begin to question their own motivations for drinking and begin to see that they are frequently losing control, and that they often suffer harsh consequences from their drinking. Ted, for instance, has had fights while drinking, he has been ejected from bars, and he has come to work hung over from his alcohol use the previous night. These consequences, and his perception of a strong need for alcohol, prompted him to spontaneously decide during the interview that he was an alcoholic.[4]

> TOM: Have you ever thought you might have some problems with alcohol?
>
> TED: Yes. Definitely. I'm an alcoholic, almost positive I am. I'm sure I am. . . . I feel the need to drink sometimes quite strongly. . . . My father, he's an alcoholic. Yeah, I think I can probably admit [it] right now. I do think about it. It bothers me that it has control of me, but I also am hoping that the mind is strong enough with the potential it has, that I will be able to stop.

The consequences of drinking were even more severe for Chuck. When asked if he had ever thought he might have some problems with alcohol, he replied, "Yes, all the time, because I've attempted suicide a couple of times because of alcohol, or along with alcohol, I should say. And just the way I feel, you know, my body. The next day I'll go, 'God! I can't keep doing this every day'."

What happens to most men who eventually label themselves as alcoholics is that they begin to drink by themselves more and more frequently, gradually withdrawing from social drinking situations. Three of the four self-identified alcoholics who were still drinking not only drank every day, but they also frequently drank alone. This is a critical factor in the self-labeling process because with increased solitary drinking, the individual is deprived of a group that he can use to normalize his consumption, and thus may be more likely to view his drinking as pathological. On the other hand, an individual who is drinking heavily, but within a heavily drinking social group, would find it very difficult to conceptualize his own behavior as anything other than ordinary.

One might think that after an individual labels himself as an alcoholic, attempts at sobriety would naturally follow. This is not necessarily the case, however. Despite their definition of self as alcoholic, many men have not done very much about terminating their drinking.

> TOM: What have you done about [your drinking]?
>
> TED: Probably nothing, not much. Simply because I'm so addicted, so comfortable with the beers at night when I come home.

To understand how men begin to take action, I now turn to an examination of those respondents who are currently abstinent. The self-identified recovering alcoholics have decided to terminate drinking. They have joined AA and are attempting to live alcohol-free.

Self-identified Recovering Alcoholics

The drinking histories of the recovering alcoholics in this study are the most instructive in understanding alcoholism as a career. Not only have they come to a point when they are attempting to remain abstinent, but they also show more insight about their problems than do the other men. This may be the result of their participation in AA and similar programs. Often these respondents use the language of AA to describe their past behavior and their present situation. Although the backgrounds of these men vary, there are a number of commonalities in their drinking patterns and related experiences. In the following section I examine how they began to drink and how they lost control of their drinking, paying special attention to their perceptions of their behavior and the interaction they have had with others.

Drinking Careers

The recovering alcoholics had been drinking for a long time. They began using alcohol as teenagers (their age at first consistent alcohol use ranged from 12 to 20 years) and continued drinking for a median time of 12.5 years (with a range of 8 to 42 years). Their mean time of alcohol use was 17.4 years. Like most people, these men began to drink in social situations. Usually, this was with high school or college friends; sometimes drinking began during military service. Alcohol use and consequent problems seem to have increased while the men were in the military.

Transitions in behavior and related self-definitions are not easily made. The drinking career is a slow process during which changes occur so subtly that they are not usually noted by the individual. The realization that one's drinking is different comes slowly, with the perception that one's alcohol use is no longer socially motivated. As Todd said, "In the beginning you don't even think about [drinking], but at the end I knew I had a drinking problem, and I was still drinking." His experiences illustrate this process. Todd first began using alcohol consistently at the age of twenty, when he "moved in with some people who had access and were fairly heavy drinkers themselves." At the time, he "really didn't think about [drinking]. It was just done." When asked about the amount he was drinking then, he replied, "I honestly don't know. I don't remember, really. We were drinking quite a bit if we were having a party at night, and other days not much at all." As he continued drinking he experienced blackouts, but he refused to deal with the implications of these physical effects. Since his alcohol use was similar to that of his companions, he was spared having to define his drinking as pathological. "Up until about maybe three or four years ago," he said, "I never really noticed that I was doing anything differently from anyone else." Eventually, however, Todd began to withdraw from his friends. "I guess I originally started going out for companionship," he said, "and [I] was drinking and continued going out, and then just increased the drinking and finally, I would stay at home, mostly." Once a person begins drinking on his own, as Todd did, the stage is set for the reevaluation of the meaning of his drinking.

Over time, the individual's alcohol consumption gradually increases in terms of both the amount used and the number of occasions during which he drinks.

> TOM: How many drinks were you having when you were drinking?
>
> KENNETH: Up to the point where I'd black out. And then I'd still drink after I'd black out.
>
> CHRIS: When I drank I was pretty serious about it, so it was not uncommon for me to have fourteen to eighteen drinks before I would experience a blackout.

Eventually, drinking becomes so central to the alcoholic's existence that he is doing it continuously. Unlike social drinkers, whose alcohol use often varies with circumstances, the problem drinker's consumption is generally consistent, regardless of what is going on around him.

> TOM: In what situations were you using alcohol?
>
> VINNIE: I couldn't really pinpoint a situation, I was drinking it all the time. I would drink it at 2:00 in the morning or 12:00 in the afternoon, 'round the clock.
>
> BARRY: I had reached the point where I didn't require a situation.

By this time, the person's motives for drinking have changed; they are no longer social. As alcohol use increases, the individual tends to isolate himself more and more when drinking, a pattern reported by all but one of these self-identified alcoholics. Even his visits to gay bars reflect his preoccupation with alcohol. As Read (1980) notes, these excursions tend to be less social than those of nonalcoholics; the men were more likely to go out alone and to avoid others when drinking:

> I started to just become basically interested in getting completely loaded, and I wasn't interested in the social scene any more. I would just go to get completely bombed. Actually, I would drink before I left for the bar, you know. I would drink quite a bit. (Vinnie)

> I usually drank at a bar, usually at the back of the bar. Or, if somebody interfered with my drinking, I would move away from them. So I avoided—ostensibly I went out, I thought, to find sexual contacts—but often it was really avoiding any contact, and just drinking. (Chris)

Toward the end of their drinking careers, the men tended to withdraw, not only from social situations, but from places where others were present, such as the bar.

> VINNIE: In the last six months I started drinking at home a lot more, all the time. I never went out to bars after that.

> TOM: How do you account for switching from, say, bar drinking to home drinking?

> VINNIE: Oh, I became totally self-obsessed. I didn't want to be around anybody; I just withdrew and took the alcohol with me.

> KENNETH: I have a big bottle of white wine in my refrigerator and I used to think about just coming home and killing that bottle of wine. Like I said, I lived alone and most of the time I'd come home alone and open a bottle of wine, get undressed, and have the wine while I was undressing and sit in front of the TV and watch Johnny Carson and sink into oblivion.

This alienation is a two-way street, involving not only pulls toward alcohol but also pushes away from others. Alcoholics tend to be rejected by former friends and associates, and for good reasons:

People couldn't be around me anymore. I mean, the last couple of months of my drinking I had two or three close friends tell me to get lost, you know. People just didn't want to be around me anymore. I would rob them, I would lie to them. . . . What happened eventually, [was that] nobody wanted to be with me because, you know, I was a con, basically a con, so they just left me alone. (Vinnie)

I was always a happy person. You know, people like me because of my particular attitudes, my brightness, my life-of-the-party type of thing, drinking or not drinking, you know. But I became a very depressed type of person. It came to the point that it was noticeable to other people. And I was very depressed myself. I sat around with a rather dejected look on my face most of the time. (Barry)

The settings in which drinking occurs also begin to change. While most gay men use alcohol socially in gay-related settings, alcoholics do not. They were the only men I interviewed who drank extensively in heterosexually oriented bars and taverns, places that are usually avoided by most gay men:

Toward the end it was mostly straight bars because I wasn't involved in sex or anything. It just became drinking, so it didn't really matter. (Vinnie)

If we went into the whole thing in depth we'd find out that I did more socializing in . . . a straight bar atmosphere rather than a gay [one]. (Barry)

These men often voiced a hostility toward other gays, and a consequent aversion to the gay bar scene:

To this day, I don't care for gay social life much. . . . I'm a gay alcoholic, but I can't stand drunks and faggots. (Barry)

I'm not fond of gay social [life]. . . . I honestly don't feel comfortable in [gay] bars. I don't like their clothes, I don't like their hairstyles, I don't like their looks, and I'm not comfortable. I feel really hostile in [them] and almost vindictive. (Joel)

Part of the explanation for the alienation of these men from others lies in their participation in secondary deviance. Once they have assumed the alcoholic role, their lives revolve around drinking.

They avoid others who might criticize their behavior and when they do interact with others, it is only with heavy drinkers. This is typical not only of gays but also of many other heavy drinkers. Cahalan (1970) found that a group of drinkers with high problem drinking scores had a favorable or tolerant attitude toward drinking and high scores on a scale of environmental supports for drinking, which included factors such as friends and associates who drank a lot, friends with drinking problems, and people close to them who would find their heavy drinking acceptable: "The few friends, and I do mean a few, were generally alcoholic. Looking back, I can recognize their condition—whether they recognized it or not is something else. But I think I actually chose to associate with people who drank a lot" (Chris). These men sometimes rob their friends and lie to them as Vinnie has related, and they may even engage in criminal activities to support their habit:

> I used to go down to the supermarket when I stopped going to bars and change price tags in the Safeway. . . . And I didn't have enough money and I used to go down . . . and get some Grand Marnier, and it was very expensive. . . . I used to change the price tags from $9.00 and I used to put a $3.00 price tag on it. And it was a small bottle and the cashiers . . . weren't familiar with that alcohol in particular, so they rang it up for $3.00 because the bottle was small, and that was my rationalization. (Vinnie)

At some point, alcohol use begins to spill over to situations from which it had previously been segregated. As a professional photographer reported:

> I was getting the habit. I was drinking before I'd go on a job, too, which I thought was bad. And at weddings, where there was a lot of booze on bars and things, I would drink. And I had a feeling that this was known, although it didn't affect anything. (Barry)

> And sometimes I'd be drinking at work, too. I worked at a store and I could slip into the back of the stockroom. I worked in a drugstore with a large liquor department—one of the great ironies of my life—they put me in charge of that whole liquor room that was downstairs and was in a cage. I was in charge of it and had the inventory. And I could go down and break a half-pint of vodka and it would go into "breakage." Then I would drink the broken bottle.

> So, I could drink a lot. And I was in charge of the store. So, I drank a lot in the store, stole a lot, too. (Joel)

It is apparent that under the influence of alcohol, the men quoted above were risk takers. An interesting phenomenon pointed out by a number of these self-avowed alcoholics was a perceived relationship among their alcoholic bouts, the search for sexual partners, and a need to court danger. They often put themselves in situations where their safety and lives were jeopardized:

> Oh, the bizarre behavior—picking up people who somehow, if I were sober, I'd know intuitively that this wasn't a person I'd want to be with. But in a drunken state, those people seem to be chosen. I guess what I'm saying is the intuition would still be working, but instead of repelling, it was attracting. Because I found myself in a number of situations where I really often wanted to die, and since I was too chicken to do it myself, I was often putting myself in an environment where that would be accomplished for me by someone else. . . . So, anyway, that happened several times. For some reason, in a moment of clarity, I was able to run. And then I got robbed several times, rolled. There were a number of incidents where something really horrible should have happened, and for some reason something intervened and I was once again saved. (Chris)

The difference between these recovering alcoholics and the self-identified alcoholics who were still drinking lies in their perceptions of the consequences of their behavior. As Ray (1961) points out, cycles of abstinence are typically initiated when the individual questions his or her addict identity

> and examines it in all of its implications and ramifications. . . . An episode of cure begins in the private thoughts of the addict rather than in his overt behavior. These deliberations develop as a result of experience in specific situations of interaction with important others that cause the addict to experience social stress, to develop some feeling of alienation from or dissatisfaction with his present identity. . . . (p. 134).

Vinnie illustrates how rejection by others becomes part of this process. It does not, however, necessarily precipitate an immediate attempt at abstention, nor is it the only factor:

I remember the thing that scared me the most, that triggered it the most, [was when] a couple of my friends told me to get lost. They basically told me to get out of their lives. And I didn't react to that, you know. I had no more feelings left. It didn't matter to me that my friends, these so-called good friends, told me to leave. And that's what scared me the most, was that I just walked away. . . . I didn't care at all. And I knew that there was something wrong, something was going on deeper than I ever had any experience with.

Abstinence often occurred after a particularly traumatic experience whose implications were suddenly realized by the individual in a way that similar situations had never been examined before. Such situations become turning points that propel the individual to take stock and to attempt to stop, rather than to merely control, his drinking. The crucial variables in this process are the individual's self-definitions as they are affected by his perceptions of the social contexts in which he participates, and his interpretations of his interactions with others.

In his discussion of "hitting bottom," Rudy (1986) points out that people who become involved with AA typically do so in association "with some sudden crisis which occurred as a direct or indirect result of drinking. The most typical crisis involves behavior that the drinker defines as unacceptable or intolerable" (p. 22). Such was the case among the men I interviewed. Alcohol use was terminated, and help from organizations such as Gay AA was sought only after particularly dramatic turning points, such as when the individual realized he had endangered his life or that of others. For example, Joel said that he decided to stay sober after having been beaten senseless and robbed by two rough men whom he had brought home. After gaining consciousness, he realized that he had unthinkingly jeopardized the life of his grandmother who lived alone in the apartment below his:

And I was done. At least there was somehow a feeling, "I cannot live this way. I can't face that any more. Any of it." And, of course, I knew about AA. And my aunt came over and the police came. And [my friend] said something about, "You know where there's help." I knew I needed help, so I went to a meeting. I've been sober since.

Chris identified two situations that precipitated two separate attempts at sobriety, including the present sober period. In the first of these, another man induced Chris to beat and rob him. Chris attacked the man so savagely that he was hospitalized. In the more recent case, Chris attempted, while intoxicated, to run down a motorcyclist. Fortunately, he failed to hit the man, but was himself injured in the subsequent crash:[5]

> Toward the end the bizarre behavior came back. I chased a motorcycle one night and almost caught it. You know, it could have been deadly. And that was again another turning point. I realized that I had lost control again, and fortunately again nobody was hurt or killed, but I knew I wasn't any more in control [using beer] than I had been under the vodka. (Chris)

Sometimes, a dangerous situation occurred during a blackout. Both the severity and the perceived implications of blackouts, rather than their number, were related to taking action about one's alcohol use:

> I was driving home from this party . . . and it was very, very foggy, and I don't even remember getting in the car. . . . All I can remember is opening my eyes, looking at my friend sitting next to me in the car, and she's yelling and screaming for me to slow down the car. . . . And I looked ahead of me and there was this big truck. It was like I was dreaming, and I closed my eyes and the next thing I remember is hitting the curb outside my house. . . . [The next morning] we went out and looked at my car and there was a big dent in it. And I asked her if I had hit a person and she said no, she didn't remember. It was then and there that I realized that . . . I could very well have killed myself and killed her or killed someone else. I was driving home in a car I didn't even know I was in. It was then that I made myself believe that I needed help. . . . That's when I called AA. (Kenneth)

Barry's last attempt at sobriety began after he experienced a bout of violent nausea in which blood was mixed with his vomit. At that point, he began to examine his drinking:

> Then I was getting bad feelings of depression all the time, and it was just so bad that I [had] just had it. . . . I mean, I wasn't able to cope with my problems because of the damn booze . . . but when

I get right down to it, I couldn't do anything about it, and so I stopped drinking. I just made that decision. It would just get worse rather than better. (Barry)

Even when someone makes a sincere attempt to abstain from alcohol, he does not necessarily stop permanently. All of the men reported having gone through more than one cycle of abstinence and relapse. Barry relapsed after an abstinent period of four months when a close friend came to visit. They were in a pool, exposed to the sun, and it was hot so he decided to have a beer. Other beers followed. After his friend died suddenly from a massive heart attack, Barry began to drink heavily again, "and it kind of flipped me out, I guess, too. That's why I started drinking heavy, probably heavier than I did before."

Joel reported that he went through "periodic reformations." Among other things, his relapses were triggered by problems with his lover. His lover was also an alcoholic, whom Joel describes as a "hustler." Chris came closest to providing a sociological explanation for his relapse, observing that his feelings about himself and his identity had not changed during his abstinent period.

TOM: Why did you resume drinking after that period?
CHRIS: I don't think I had any basis for not drinking. I didn't have any good feelings about myself. I still viewed myself in the same light and hadn't taken any moves to change that perspective. . . . It just didn't work, because I wasn't changing anything; I was just stopping drinking. So all I was was a sober piece of shit, rather than a sober person.

Chris makes two critical points in this statement. First, he points out that he suffered from low self-esteem. This is characteristic of these recovering alcoholics; all of them said that they had had low self-esteem when they were drinking. These men are not unique in having such problems, which they share with many heterosexual problem drinkers (Connor, 1962). Smith (1982) notes that "low self-esteem is frequently an evident symptom in both alcoholics and gay males" (p. 57). The following comments further illustrate the problem:

It was easier and less expensive to drink at home. I felt so bad about myself, I had such low self-worth that I couldn't face people, so naturally I stayed at home. (Vinnie)

If somebody said something that offended me, one sharp remark, or somebody turned to me and said, "Why don't you lay off?"—that was instant destruction. I was exposed. I was steaming, and away I'd go. The first little hint in a gay or straight bar of anyone who was hostile to me, and I'd clear out. (Joel)

Second, Chris notes that he had not reconceptualized himself as a nondrinker. In order for someone to successfully abstain from alcohol, there must be a fundamental reconceptualization of self as the kind of person who does not drink. This is obviously a difficult undertaking, given the length of time the problem drinker has been using alcohol, the ubiquity of the beverage, and the favorable attitudes toward its use within the larger society. For gay men, living without alcohol is particularly difficult because drinking is an integral part of the gay world. Leaving alcohol may also mean leaving an established group of friends. This does not seem to have been a difficult problem for these men, however, because they had long since alienated their friends and withdrawn from their social groups. Their most recent drinking companions were acquaintances or "bar buddies," rather than close friends.

TOM: Do your friends drink a lot or not?

TODD: Up until three months ago, I didn't have many friends, mostly acquaintances. I would say, yes, they did. Now, it's about a thirty-seventy mix: thirty that do drink quite a bit, and maybe seventy that drink occasionally or rarely. . . . What I am trying to do is [find] a social life that is not based on bars. And I think, you know, for working at it a month, I've made amazing progress.

KENNETH: This is the point in my life where I'm separating my friends from my drinking friends. My drinking friends don't understand [why I'm no longer drinking]. My friends who know I had a problem understand and support me very much.

Reference group change is a critical variable in maintaining sobriety. The most effective groups appear to be those composed of former drinkers who are themselves attempting to remain alcohol-free. Within these groups the individual finds an unconditional welcome and emotional support from people who understand his or her problems because they have faced the same issues themselves. The former drinker is given opportunities to develop a self-image as an abstainer by verbalizing the sober values that are reinforced by the group:

> And I saw the listing for the 10:00 Saturday morning Step Study at the [AA] for gays, and I thought, "Should I go or shouldn't I go?" I said, "Shit, I'll go," and I went and I really enjoyed it. There were people there who were sharing experiences just like mine. People who didn't understand if their drinking was the cause of their homosexuality, or if their homosexuality was the cause of their drinking. For whichever was the cause, they were alcoholics, and they were admitting it. And they were trying to do something with their lives, and that's exactly what I was doing. The same situation and the same environment and the same people. (Kenneth)

> I went to a meeting. And they were very nice and I liked them and I felt good right away with those people. And I did what AA said, and I started going to other meetings downtown, and I didn't drink. I was feeling better, and I got things back together. (Joel)

The longer individuals stay with the group, the more they become integrated into it. With integration comes commitment to the norms and values of the group. Eventually, the recovering alcoholic develops what Hirschi (1969) calls commitment to conventional lines of action. A commitment to others, with a consequent commitment to their values, is an important insulator from deviance. This growing commitment to conformity was illustrated by two AA members.

> TOM: What do you think is keeping you sober right now?

> CHRIS: I think doing what I have to do, which is continue to try to grow with myself as a person relating to other people. Be helpful when I can to a person with an alcohol problem. Continue my spiritual growth, and that's it. Maintain my conscious contact with God.

> BARRY: I'm at the point where I feel I can't drink now, all those people would be so disappointed. I have a responsibility to them.

The men's sober comportment reflects how difficult it is for them to maintain sobriety, even while involved in a group to which they

want to conform. The patterns of drinking that were established
when they were using alcohol heavily become so ingrained in these
men that they continue the same patterns, even when they are
sober: "I'm doing just about the same lifestyle as I did before, when
I was drinking heavy, and I haven't changed anything since I've
stopped drinking. It's just the fact that I don't drink alcohol" (Barry).
Chris was even more explicit in explaining the behavioral carryover
from alcohol use to drinking nonalcoholic beverages:

> I think my [sober drinking] pattern is probably pretty much like
> my other pattern: going to multiple bars drinking. And sober, I still
> barhop. I find myself with mineral water or any liquid, drinking
> the same way I drank alcoholic drinks in a bar. In other words, the
> drink wouldn't last very long. I could go through a Perrier in thirty-
> two seconds.

In order to maintain sobriety, individuals must go through a
transitional process. First, they have to leave the drinking group.
Then, they must be integrated into a group whose goals emphasize
abstinence. Next, they must have an opportunity to verbalize and
demonstrate sober values, and finally, they must receive rewards
for sobriety: "I haven't [been depressed] since I've not been drinking.
Well, towards the beginning, maybe. But I feel great. Because I'm
looking forward to doing things I want to do. At least I have goals
now. I didn't before. Maybe that was depressing, too" (Barry). Ultimately, what should occur is a reconceptualization of self as nondrinker.

Alcoholism and Sexual Orientation

While the drinking histories of gay problem drinkers are
similar to those of their heterosexual counterparts, they are different
in one important respect. In attempting to account for their heavy
alcohol use, some of the men have developed a rationale that appears
to be unique to gays, that is, their difficulty in expressing their
sexual identities. They felt that their inability to deal with their
sexual orientation was involved in their abuse of alcohol. This is not
uncommon. Smith (1982), for example, points out that "being gay
has often been used by alcohol abusers as an excuse to continue

047 4700047 470000 470000 4

drinking" (p. 56). Small and Leach (1977) also note that almost all of the alcoholics in their study had used their homosexuality as an excuse for drinking. This rationale was expressed by some of the men I interviewed:

> I don't know if I was drinking because I was a homosexual or a bisexual, or if my homosexuality was caused by my drinking, or if my drinking was caused by my homosexuality. I did know for a fact that I was sexually attracted to men, and that society does not accept that, as a whole. And to deal with my internal problems I would drink. . . . I was drinking because I was unhappy with myself, that I wasn't being motivated to make something of my life. (Kenneth)

> My reason for drinking some of the time was because I was gay. I was highly pissed at God, both because I was caught up in the drinking and because I was gay. And notice I again didn't say I was alcoholic because I don't think at that period of time I considered myself one. (Chris)

There is an extensive psychoanalytic literature on the hypothesized relationship between alcoholism and homosexuality. However, as I noted in chapter 1, the research findings on this topic are contradictory and confusing. This does not, of course, prevent men from justifying their alcoholism by blaming it on their sexual orientation; the recovering alcoholics, at least, did have some difficulties in coming to terms with their sexuality. For example, although Barry now says, "Oh, I'm quite comfortable being gay. . . . I really like myself as a person," this reflects a recent change in his feelings that seems to have developed as a result of his current sobriety and as a result of setting achievable goals. Vinnie appears to be more typical of the men who blame their alcohol use on their sexuality. Although he came out at about the age of thirteen, he indicated that he still has not accepted his sexual orientation. "I don't know how I feel about sex," he said. "You know, it's confusing to me."

In this chapter, I have examined the careers of gay problem drinkers. In explaining how men come to define themselves as alcoholics and how they make the decision to stop drinking, I developed a typology of three different categories of problem drinkers. I called the first group of men researcher-identified problem drinkers because they scored in the moderately heavy to heavy range on the modified Quantity-Frequency Index. All of them reported having had numerous alcohol-related difficulties, and their behavior caused concern among their friends. In addition, they all reported instances of solitary drinking and of alcohol use while depressed, and said that alcohol consumption was increasingly the primary motivation behind their behavior. Despite this, they were reluctant to label themselves as alcoholics. They resisted the label by emphasizing they were drinking because they wanted to, and they felt that as long as they could control their alcohol use, they had no real problems.

The next group of men were self-identified alcoholics who were still drinking. It took these men a long time to define themselves in this way for two reasons. First, there is a widespread acceptance both of heavy drinking and of certain kinds of alcohol-influenced behavior, such as being loud and unruly, within the men's social circles. The men could therefore escape self-definition as alcoholic as long as this behavior could be explained as being an expected normal part of celebrating, partying, and the like. Second, men tend to consume alcohol similarly to the way their friends do, and in comparable amounts. Only after withdrawing from their friends and beginning to engage in solitary drinking are the men able to perceive their alcohol use as possibly pathological. Physical symptoms are sometimes the precipitating causes that begin the self-labeling process.

During their long drinking careers, the recovering alcoholics gradually increased the frequency and quantity of their consumption. As alcohol became central to their lives, they managed to alienate those close to them. They engaged in secondary deviance, including stealing from their friends, their employers, and even from their own businesses, to continue their drinking. They wrote checks with insufficient funds and ran up their lines of credit. Two of the men told me that they even cached money in the bars they frequented and would frantically tear up floorboards in the bathrooms and look in the toilet paper holders for cash they might have hidden. They were arrested for public intoxication and for driving while intoxicated. They engaged in high-risk activities that frequently jeopardized their own lives as well as those of other people. Long before this time, they were experiencing blackouts but would nevertheless continue drinking. The recovering alcoholics finally reached a point when they felt they had to stop drinking. These turning points usually came with the realization that they could not go on as they had been. They joined AA or similar organizations and began the process of redefining themselves as nondrinkers. They still had issues to deal with, including low self-esteem and ambivalence over their sexual identities.

9. Alternative Explanations for Gay Problem Drinking

As I have emphasized in the previous chapters, drinking is an integral part of the gay scene. Many gay men are alcohol users, and of these a substantial proportion can be characterized as problem drinkers. How is one to account for the ubiquity of alcohol in the gay male subculture? One popular explanation used by a number of researchers is that heavy drinking is at least partially the result of alienation, a state which is seen as characteristic of gays. For example, Fifield (1975) claims that gay people experience a high degree of alienation and that "these feelings of alienation in turn will contribute to a high rate of alcohol abuse among the gay population" (p. 57). She admits, however, that she was not able to establish a causal relationship between the two variables. Nevertheless, she asserts that "alienation is a strong contributing factor in the high alcohol abuse rate for gay bar users" (p. 46). This theme is reiterated in her later research (Fifield, Lathan, & Phillips, 1977). Similarly, Ziebold and Mongeon (1982) point out that "gay people drink and party to hide from the world, to escape their feelings of being different. . . . Accepting this view of themselves, the victims accumulate more guilt and more of an urge to escape into drinking" (pp. 5–6).

Nardi (1982b) emphasizes that for men coming out into the gay world, alcohol use can serve as one means of coping with a perceived oppressive social situation and the stress stemming from identity

126

problems. Additionally, he feels that "the absence of significant, subculturally valued alternatives to drinking settings, especially in the smaller, less urban centers, contributes to the dependency on alcohol as an acceptable solution to feelings of anxiety, alienation, and low self-esteem" (p. 21).[1] Lohrenz et al. (1978) identify social and psychological pressures and family problems as contributing to heavy drinking.

The alienation explanation for gay drinking proposed by these writers is not adequate, and these difficulties are especially apparent in Fifield's (1975) work. First, the concept of alienation is presented in a sloppy and cavalier manner, which is not a problem unique to writers concerned with drinking and homosexuality. According to Hughes (1979), "Alienation is one of those concepts, which have tended to abound in sociology, used to describe and explain almost any kind of social behaviour and usually succeeding in describing and explaining nothing" (p. 4). Seeman (1959) writes that alienation, "a concept that is so central in sociological work, and so clearly laden with value implications, demands special clarity" (p. 783). The writers on gay drinking assume that the meaning of the concept is obvious. However, alienation has several different meanings.

A second problem, which is related to the first, is that different kinds of alienation are used, and confused, in the same passage, without any attempt to distinguish among them. Furthermore, some types of alienation are ignored. For example, at times Fifield (and others) appear to use alienation as synonymous with estrangement from family members and/or from the norms and values of the nongay world. I have coined the term *interpersonal alienation* to refer to the former usage, while the latter type of alienation has been called *isolation* (Seeman, 1959, pp. 788–89). At other times, however, alienation appears as a personal, internalized social psychological state, perhaps caused by the first kind of alienation and characterized by feelings of detachment from self as well as from others, which Seeman (1959) terms *self-estrangement* (pp. 789–90). Other forms of alienation, such as *powerlessness*, (pp. 784–85), *meaninglessness* (pp. 785–86) and *normlessness* (pp. 787–88) seem to be ignored.

A third problem found in writings on gays and alienation is that the researchers do not specify the mechanisms through which alienation results in alcohol abuse. To imply that rejection by family and heterosexual society somehow results in a feeling of being different, which in turn causes people to escape into drinking, is not an explanation. Why does rejection (if it does occur uniformly in all cases) cause individuals to become alienated? And why must this alienation cause heavy drinking? How is one to account for problem drinkers who claim not to have been previously alienated from their significant others? How does one explain the fact that some gays who have been rejected have been and continue to be abstainers or light or moderate drinkers?

A fourth problem most writers on alienation have is that they view this concept as an either/or phenomenon. In fact, alienation may be viewed as a matter of degree, with only the heaviest or alcoholic drinkers being in that state. Some writers seem not to make a distinction between ordinary social drinkers, heavy drinkers, problem drinkers, alcoholics, and the like. In this view, all gay people who drink are alienated. There are, however, exceptions to this position. For example, Smith (1982) argues that "viewing the gay man as isolated and lonely is not very accurate; however, the view of the drinking alcoholic as alienated is often quite accurate" (p. 65).[2] The present study supports Smith's position. It was the problem drinkers, rather than the social drinkers, who reported being alienated from others. As I noted in chapter 8, a good deal of this alienation was of their own making. They were rejected by their gay friends after having taken advantage of them in various ways.

A final difficulty with the way in which the alienation concept is used is that it ignores the importance of alternative groups to the individual as both sources of attraction and as reference points for his or her own behavior. People are not always rejected or forced out by their families; instead, they often leave to explore their sexuality on their own terms. The gay world, therefore, frequently serves as a positive attraction for many individuals. People seek out and find new groups, albeit with some trepidation. But as opposed to being permanently alienated in some vague sense, many gay people do become quite well integrated into supportive friendship groups.

Alienation as a Concept

Clarity is important in considering the impact of alienation on gay drinking. The idea of alienation as a human condition has been part of the social science literature for a long time. It can be traced back to Hegel and to Marx's modification of his ideas (Hughes, 1979). For Marx, alienation was a structural feature of modern industrial society. Human beings, who are naturally creative in a simpler world, give up control over their own destiny in an industrial society. They are then controlled by forces outside of themselves, such as by the owners of the enterprises in which they work. They become alienated from themselves, as well as from the products of their own labor. The Marxian conceptualization incorporates such social psychological aspects as self-estrangement and powerlessness into alienation, although these states of being are caused by the social structure.

In an attempt to clarify and operationalize alienation, Seeman (1959) distinguishes five ways in which the concept has been used. He examines these meanings from the viewpoint of the actor, which is compatible with the symbolic interactionist perspective taken in the present research. The first meaning distinguished by Seeman is powerlessness, defined as "the expectancy or probability held by the individual that his own behavior cannot determine the occurrence of the outcomes, or reinforcements, he seeks" (p. 784). The second usage of alienation is meaninglessness, which "refers to the individual's sense of understanding the events in which he is engaged. We may speak of high alienation, in the meaningless usage, when *the individual is unclear as to what he ought to believe—when the individual's minimal standards for clarity in decision-making are not met*" [Seeman's italics] (p. 786). In other words, the individual cannot make predictions about the outcomes of acting on a given belief. The third conceptualization of alienation is normlessness, which is derived from Durkheim's (1897/1951) description of "anomy," a state in which

> society is disturbed by some painful crisis or by beneficient but abrupt transitions [so that] it is momentarily incapable of exercising [an] influence [on its members]. . . . All regulation is lacking for a time. The limits are unknown between the possible and the impossible, what is just and what is unjust. . . . Traditional rules [of society] have lost their authority. (pp. 252–53)

This concept, according to Seeman, has been "over-extended to include a wide variety of both social conditions and psychic states: personal disorganization, cultural breakdown, reciprocal distrust, and so on" (p. 787). Looking at anomy (normlessness) from the individual's perspective, and taking his cue from Merton's (1949) development of the concept,[3] Seeman defines it as a situation "in which there is a high expectancy that socially unapproved behaviors are required to achieve given goals" (p. 788).

Seeman's fourth type of alienation is isolation. He defines this type of alienation in terms of "reward values: The alienated in the isolation sense are those who . . . *assign low reward value to goals or beliefs that are typically highly valued in the given society*" [Seeman's italics] (pp. 788–89). This is not the same thing, Seeman writes, as "a lack of 'social adjustment'—of the warmth, security, or intensity of an individual's social contacts" (p. 788). It is just that the individual has become estranged from some of the popularly accepted standards of society. So, for example, gay men may feel detached from societal expectations of marriage and raising children, or from norms of sexual monogamy, and thus create their own cultural norms and values.[4] The fifth type of alienation distinguished by Seeman is self-estrangement, which he characterizes as

> the loss of intrinsically meaningful satisfactions. . . . One way to state such a meaning is to see alienation as *the degree of dependence of the given behavior upon anticipated future rewards* [Seeman's italics], that is, upon rewards that lie outside the activity itself. . . . In this view, what has been called self-estrangement refers essentially to the inability of the individual to find self-rewarding . . . activities that engage him. (p. 790)

Dean (1961) conceives of alienation as having three major components: powerlessness, normlessness, and social isolation. Using scales constructed to measure these components, he found that they strongly correlated with one another. Dean's use of powerlessness is similar to Seeman's construction. His discussion of normlessness, however, is somewhat different. He distinguishes between two subcategories of normlessness. The first, which he calls *purposelessness*, he defines, quoting MacIver (1950, pp. 84–87), as "the absence of values that might give purpose or direction to life, the loss of intrinsic and socialized values, the insecurity of the hopelessly disoriented" (p. 754). Purposelessness appears to be similar to Seeman's concept of self-estrangement. The second component of normlessness is described as a conflict of norms. Finally, Dean sees social isolation as including both isolation from group standards and a feeling of separation from the group. This conceptualization includes both Seeman's notion of isolation and what I have called interpersonal alienation.

Alienation and Drinking

In the present research, several dimensions of alienation are examined as they may be related to the men's drinking behavior. Questions asked of respondents fell under the categories of interpersonal alienation, isolation, self-estrangement, and powerlessness.[5] Additionally, two measures of drinking involvement were developed as independent variables to be used in correlating measures of alienation with alcohol use. The first of these (quanfreq) was based on respondents' scores on the modified Quantity-Frequency Index. The second measure of drinking (probdrnk) was based on the categorization of drinking involvement discussed in chapter 8, which ranged from nonproblem drinkers to researcher-identified problem drinkers to self-identified alcoholics who were still drinking to presently abstinent alcoholics. These two independent variables correlate quite strongly ($r = .61$, $p<.05$), which is not too surprising since an individual's score on the modified Quantity-Frequency Index was one of several variables I considered when I categorized him on the probdrnk measure.[6] They are, however, quite distinct, because the quanfreq variable is simply a straightforward measure of alcohol consumption, while the probdrnk variable incorporates measures of problem drinking, such as having been arrested for alcohol-related offenses, loss of jobs, ejection from bars, fights with lovers, illnesses resulting from drinking, and so forth. An individual could, theoretically, score high on the quanfreq variable but low on the probdrnk variable if he has few social or medical consequences related to his alcohol consumption. Sixteen men who scored in the moderately heavy category on the modified Quantity-Frequency Index were classified as nonproblem drinkers on the probdrnk variable.[7]

Interpersonal Alienation

Interpersonal alienation, the estrangement from others, was examined in a number of different ways that were conceptualized into three subsets of questions. For the interpersonal intimacy sub-set, the men were asked about the number of really close friends they had in the Paradise City area whom they talked to about their most intimate feelings, and the number of people with whom they could share a significant event in their lives. The familial relations subset included questions about where their families resided, how often they were in contact with their families, and how close they felt toward parents and siblings. The geographic mobility subset was used in order to get some measure of transiency, a factor that can be related to interpersonal alienation. The men were asked where they grew up, how long they had been living in Paradise City, with whom they were presently living, and whether they knew their neighbors and were friendly with them.

Interpersonal intimacy.   When the men were asked about the number of really close friends they had in Paradise City, it quickly became apparent that most of them were involved in friend-ship networks: 18% had one or two friends, 27% had three to five friends, 33% had six to ten friends, and 22% reported that they had more than ten friends living in the area. A number of respondents made it clear that they included both heterosexual and homosexual friends within their intimate circles. There was no significant correla-tion between the number of friends and either of my measures of alcohol involvement.

The men were asked, If something very significant happened in your life, how many people are there in the Paradise City area with whom you could share this? Only one man said that he had no one with whom to share an important event; 9% said that they had one or two people they could talk with; 35% identified between three and five individuals; 22% said they could discuss things with between six and ten people; and 24% of the respondents said they could talk with more than ten people. Nine percent of the men said that the number of people with whom they could share something significant depended on what it was that had happened to them. Others with whom the men would communicate included close friends (80%), relatives (15%), lovers (15%), acquaintances (11%), coworkers (7%), roommates (4%), friends in AA (4%), teachers (2%), neighbors (2%) and pastors (2%).[8]

Although raw numbers of close friends may have some bearing on interpersonal alienation, the nature of one's relationships with them, particularly the degree of intimacy and emotional involvement felt toward others, is a more accurate indicator of alienation. There-fore, the men were asked about the quality of their interactions with others. When respondents were asked with whom they talked about their most intimate feelings, they identified a wide variety of others, some of whom were professional listeners, rather than intimate friends. So, for example, 9% of the men confided in therapists, 7% talked with their pastors, and one man shared his feelings with his teacher. Exactly half of the respondents confided in close friends, 18% talked with lovers, 13% discussed feelings with relatives, 9% communicated with roommates, 9% spoke with former lovers, and 4% looked to out-of-town friends for support.[9] The most interesting responses were from the 17% of respondents who claimed that they did not confide in others.

> Tom: Whom do you usually talk to about your most intimate feelings?

> Kevin: Myself. When I'm drunk. Persons? I can't think of any particular person. Different kinds of things, I talk to different people. That's one of my difficult things. I don't have any really deep friends like that.

> Bruce: I really don't have anybody that I could tell my most intimate thoughts to, when you get right down to it.

> Jack: I'd have to say no one, in all reality. You just can't—you've got to know someone a long time and build up a lot of respect for them, and vice versa, before you can really come out with them.

Not surprisingly, these men all drank heavily and had problems with alcohol. Whether or not one has people with whom one can share intimate feelings correlates strongly with the extent of one's drinking; heavy drinkers do not communicate with others ($r = .27$, $p < .05$).

Familial relations. Since gay people are sometimes not ac-cepted by their families because of their sexual orientations (Wein-berg, 1983), I was interested in how relationships with family mem-bers might affect drinking. Some researchers, of course, have speculated that family problems are causal factors in gay drinking (Lohrenz et al., 1978). Often gays want little to do with their families. For instance, Smith and Schneider (1981) found that only about one-fourth of the 124 gays in a hospital alcoholism rehabilitation program wanted their families involved in their treatment. However, when the men in the present study were asked how close they felt toward their parents, it was apparent that alienation from parents was not the usual situation: 52% reported feeling very close to parents, 21% said they were close, and 27% of the men said they were not close at all. Closeness with parents did not correlate significantly with either of the measures of drinking involvement. Reports on closeness to siblings were similar: 39% of the men said they were very close to their siblings, 33% said they were close, and 28% indicated that they were not close at all. Again, closeness with siblings was not significantly correlated with the measures of drinking involvement.

The respondents were asked about the frequency of contact they had with their families. As might be predicted from their responses to questions about closeness, the majority of men had frequent contact with their families: 61% communicated with family members at least once a week, 9% had contact with them two or three times a month, 14% said they communicated about once a month, and 16% were in touch with their families less than once a month. Of course, the mere fact that respondents communicate with family members does not indicate anything about the nature of this contact; it is quite possible for someone to have frequent contact with family members and yet feel distant from them:

> I call my mother about once a week, and I see her about once every two weeks on the average. Maybe once every three weeks. It's not real pleasant, but I do it out of duty. I see my younger sister about six times a year; I see my older brother about three times a year; I see my older sister maybe once a year, my other sister once every three or four years. . . . I rarely see my little brother or my other brother. The less I see my family the better I like it, except my younger sister and my older sister—we get along fairly well. (Daniel)

There was no significant correlation between frequency of contact with family members and either of the measures of drinking involvement.

Finally, respondents were asked where their families lived. Forty-four percent of respondents had relatives living in the Paradise City area. There was a significant correlation between scores on the modified Quantity-Frequency Index and family residence: the heavier drinkers did not have family living within Paradise City (r = .34, $p<.05$). This is consistent with Smith and Schneider's (1981) finding that only one-quarter of their gay alcoholic sample had families living in the same area.

Geographic mobility. Geographic mobility has been associated with a decrease in social intimacy (Berelson & Steiner, 1964), which may be related to feelings of interpersonal alienation. Smith and Schneider (1981) found that the gay alcoholics in their sample had "short term relationships, frequent moves and several job changes" (p. 133). I was therefore interested in whether or not the respondents had grown up in Paradise City, and the length of time they had been living in that community. Twenty-six percent of the men had grown up in Paradise City, although they had not necessarily been born there. There was a significant relationship between having grown up in Paradise City and the extent of a man's drinking problems: problem drinkers were less likely to have been raised in Paradise City (r = .27, $p<.05$). Apparently, living as an adult in a community in which one was raised insulates one from pathological drinking. Perhaps it is the feeling of belonging or security or the sense of having roots in a community that prevents individuals from developing drinking problems. The other side of this argument is that anonymity frees people from concerns about their reputations (and their families' reputations) and enables men who have not been raised in a particular community to engage in excessive drinking there. There was no such correlation between problem drinking and the length of time respondents had lived in Paradise City, although a large proportion of the sample (59%) had resided there for over five years. Even having been a longtime resident of a community may not be the same, in terms of identifying with a community, as having been raised there.

The other indicators of geographic mobility—whether the respondent had established a household of some sort (71% of them were living with other people) and whether they were friendly with their neighbors (68% were friendly)—were not correlated with drinking behavior.

Isolation

In order to examine isolation, or estrangement from the goals or beliefs that are typically valued in a society, the men were asked about their commitment to their religion. Sixteen percent claimed to be very strongly committed, 5% reported a strong commitment, 16% said that they were moderately committed to their religion, 5% replied that they were not very committed, and 58% said that they were not committed at all:

> The main reason I dropped [my religion] was because of the major hypocrisy that I ran into with the church. Up to that time I was . . . very devout . . . and it really made a thinker out of me. And over the years I've evolved to a point where I believe that I am, and that's it. The only divine being is within yourself, what you are, what you make of yourself, and that's my belief. You either make or break, and there's nothing out there that's going to give you this guiding hand. You'd better have it yourself or you're not going to make it. (Erik)

Although a majority of the men would appear to be alienated in the isolation sense, there was no relationship between their religious commitment and their involvement in drinking. This is somewhat different from Fisher's (1981) findings, which were based on a survey of a national probability sample. While Fisher did not relate religiosity to drinking, he did examine the relationship between religious involvement (as measured in terms of frequency of church attendance and expressed strength of the respondent's religious beliefs) and tavern attendance. He found that "the stronger one's religious involvement is, the less frequently one goes to a tavern" (p. 45).

Self-estrangement

In order to assess self-estrangement, or detachment from self and the absence of intrinsically meaningful satisfactions, the respondents were asked about their perceptions of their sexual orientations, their happiness with themselves and their lives, and their feelings of depression. When they were asked, How do you feel about being gay now?, the majority of the men (61%) replied in positive terms:

> I love it! (Daniel)

> I wouldn't want to be any other way. (Robert)

> I'm delighted! I really have no problems with being gay, and I see it in a totally different way [from when I first came out]. (Bob)

Twenty-six percent of the sample gave neutral responses to the question:

> I am gay, like I said, I'm not proud of it, I'm not ashamed of it, it's the way I am. As far as I know it's the way I was created. (Bill)

> I really don't think about it much. For me it's a fact of life. (Rodney)

> It's no big deal. (Gary)

Finally, 14% of the men said that they felt negative about being gay. While a number of the recovering alcoholics had difficulty dealing with their sexual orientation, other men also had this problem.

> Tom: How do you feel about being gay now?

> Kevin: Oh, I don't know. I have a lot of problems with it, because I don't feel that it's bringing me what I want in life.

> Adam: I still have trouble feeling it's the best way to live, where for me it's the only way to live. So I am going to make the best of it.

Feelings about being gay correlate strongly with problem drinking: the men who were most extensively affected by drinking had the most negative views of their homosexuality ($r = .32$, $p<.05$).

When the men were asked about their personal happiness, it was clear that the majority of them felt good about themselves. Forty-two percent said that they were very happy, 33% said that they were happy, 9% gave neutral responses, and 16% reported being unhappy with themselves. Problem drinkers were more likely to be unhappy with themselves than nonproblem drinkers ($r = .29$, $p<.05$).

> Tom: How happy are you with yourself as a person?

> Bruce: Not very. Not very. I do think I drink too much. I would like to find some solution to that. I find that I'm not as sympathetic and empathetic with people as I could be.

KENNETH: Not very, right now. I'm very unstable emotionally. I don't know which side to lean on. Sometimes I think it's easier just being straight, and sometimes I think it would be easier just to be gay.

Unhappiness with one's life is an indication of self-estrangement. The men, as a group, however, were satisfied with their lives. Thirty percent said that they were very happy, 26% reported being happy, 30% gave neutral responses, and 14% stated that they were unhappy. There was no significant relationship between life satisfaction and the two measures of alcohol involvement.

Finally, the possible relationship between depression and alcoholism was examined. While researchers have speculated that there may be a relationship between these two conditions, recent studies have failed to show a strong link. For example, Helzer and Przybeck (1988), who analyzed data from a large community survey of psychiatric disorders, did not find that alcoholism was any more strongly related to depression than it was to other psychiatric problems. When the men in the present study were asked if they ever became depressed, 74% of them answered affirmatively. Reasons given for depression included having business or money problems (28%), loneliness (16%), domestic or interpersonal problems (12%), and unhappiness with oneself (12%). Thirty-two percent could not identify a single precipitating factor and indicated either that depression was a constant part of their lives or an unpredictable, frequent state.

TOM: Do you ever get depressed?

VINNIE: Oh, yeah, all the time. Not nearly as much as I used to and not nearly as intense. But yes, I have [had] bad problems with depression all my life.

GARY: Oh, well, it's unpredictable. But I can notice the symptoms, the kind of behavior I do when I'm depressed and stuff. I'd say—this might sound like a lot, I don't know—but I might be depressed once a month or [once] a week.

Problem drinkers were more likely to report being depressed than were nonproblem drinkers ($r = -.28$, $p<.05$).[10]

Powerlessness

Powerlessness is the feeling that one has little control over one's situation. A way of attempting to influence the outcomes in which one has a stake is to band together with others, observing the truism that there is strength in numbers. Gay people have attempted to do this since the early 1950s, when organizations such as the Mattachine Society, the Daughters of Bilitis, and One, Inc. were founded (Adam, 1979; Yearwood & Weinberg, 1979), followed by more militant groups in the late 1960s and early 1970s. In the present study, 41% of the respondents belonged to gay or homophile groups or organizations, usually participating in more than one of them. These groups included the Gay Center, the National Gay Task Force, the Metropolitan Community Church, Dignity, Lutherans Concerned, the Gay Academic Union, the Greater Paradise City Business Association, the Gay Rights Caucus, and gay organizations linked to particular professions. All of these organizations have as part of their agendas the goal of influencing the larger society in its dealings with gay people. The men also belonged to recreational and support groups and to Gay AA. Seventy-two percent of group members said that they were active participants in these organizations. Men who belonged to homophile organizations were less likely to report being depressed than nonmembers ($r = -.31$, $p<.05$). They also appeared to be happier about their lives, although the relationship is not quite statistically significant. Membership in organizations was significantly related to both measures of drinking involvement: organization members were less likely to be heavy drinkers ($r = .41$, $p<.05$), and they were less likely to be problem drinkers ($r = .29$, $p<.05$).

In sum, the men I interviewed did not appear to be alienated, as a group, on most of the measures I examined. They seemed to be well integrated into friendship networks that often included heterosexuals as well as other gays, and they had others with whom they could share intimate feelings. They were not usually estranged from their families. Most of them were geographically stable and had established ties within Paradise City. Only in their lack of commitment to their religion did the respondents appear somewhat alienated, but they may not be any less devout than the heterosexual population.

The majority of the men reported being happy with their sexual orientation or at least accepting of it, and three-fourths of them said they were happy with themselves. Although the majority of the respondents said they were content with their lives, almost three-quarters of them did report having bouts of depression.

When measures of alcohol involvement were correlated with the measures of alienation, however, a clear pattern emerged (see table 5). The heavier drinkers and those with alcohol-related problems were more alienated than lighter and nonproblem drinkers. They did not communicate with others, and they did not have local family ties because they were more likely to have moved to Paradise City from other places. The problem drinkers felt negative about themselves and about their sexual orientation, and they were more likely to report being depressed. They did not participate in homophile organizations, which might give them greater power over their situations.

Parental Drinking

Another possible explanation for alcohol use among gays is that their drinking is the result of the influence of parental role models. In a study of thirty lesbians, half of whom were alcoholics, Schilit, Clark, and Shallenberger (1988) found that the alcoholics in their sample were more likely to report having had a parent with a drinking problem. In the present study, 83% of the respondents reported that their parents used alcohol. Specifically, 54% of them said that their fathers had problems with alcohol, and 22% stated that their mothers had drinking problems. In 13% of the cases, both parents were perceived as alcoholic:

> My father has a severe alcohol problem. He drinks first thing in the morning 'til when he goes to bed. (Michael)

> My father, I recall, you'd have to say he's an alcoholic, there's no other word for it. He lives on the stuff . . . has for as long as I can remember. That's another reason why I would never allow booze to be dominant, mainly because I always detested his veneer while he was drinking. (Erik)

Although it is certainly possible that parental drinking can affect whether and how extensively gay men use alcohol, there was no

Table 5. *Summary of Correlations Between Measures of Drinking Involvement and Measures of Alienation*

Alienation	Quanfreq	Probdrnk
I. Interpersonal alienation		
A. Interpersonal intimacy		
1. No. of close friends	.01	−.16
2. Talks to others about intimate issues	.27[a]	.23
B. Familial relations		
1. Closeness of parents	−.19	.08
2. Closeness of siblings	.13	.19
3. Freq. contact w/ family	−.07	.09
4. Family residence	.34[a]	.21
C. Geographic mobility		
1. Where grew up	.16	.27[a]
2. Time lived in P.C.	−.12	−.21
3. Living with others	.20	.06
4. Friendly with neighbors	−.18	−.07
II. Isolation		
Religious commitment	.08	.11
III. Self-estrangement		
A. Feelings about being gay	.16	.32[a]
B. Happiness with oneself	.22	.29[a]
C. Happiness with life	.16	.19
D. Feelings of depression	−.16	−.28[a]
IV. Powerlessness		
Organizational membership	.41[a]	.29[a]

Column group header: **Drinking Involvement**

[a] $p < .05$.

correlation between these variables among the men I interviewed. While 57% of the problem drinkers had at least one alcoholic parent, so did 64% of the nonproblem drinkers. Neither parental drinking nor alcoholism of either the father or the mother is significantly correlated with the men's heavy alcohol use or problem drinking. Statements such as Erik's from men whose parents are problem drinkers indicate that they became aware of some of the negative aspects of excessive consumption by observing their parents. Yet it is not clear that their perceptions of their parents' alcohol use have affected their own drinking behavior.

Reference Group Theory

A third possible explanation for the higher rate of problem drinking among gay males involves the use of reference group theory. Reference groups are groups "whose perspectives are used as a frame of reference by the actor" (Shibutani, 1955, p. 562). For Shibutani, the concept of reference group "points more to a psychological phenomenon than to an objectively existing group of men; it refers to an organization of the actor's experience. That is to say, it is a structuring of his perceptual field (p. 563)." These shared perspectives or conventional understandings held by members of social groups are, according to Shibutani, "the premises of action. . . . Those who share a common culture engage in common modes of action" (p. 564). Members of particular reference groups use their norms and values as guides for behavior. This occurs even when the other members of the group are not physically present. Even more relevant to the present study is the argument that "normative systems play a role in the consumption of alcoholic beverages" (Mizruchi & Perrucci, 1962, p. 395). A number of other writers have shown that the drinking behavior of individuals tends to be similar to that of other members of the groups to which they belong (Haer, 1955; Maddox, 1968; Prus, 1983). For most people, drinking is a social activity engaged in with friends. For example, in his study of drinking among 3,064 college students, Kraft (1981) found that 32% of his sample usually drank with one or two close friends, 40% drank with a group of close friends, and 13% used alcohol with acquaintances. Only 4% reported usually drinking with family or relatives, 3% said that they drank with whoever was around, and 1% reported solitary drinking. Seven percent were nondrinkers. As I indicated in chapter 3, social drinking was predominant for the men I interviewed; only 3 men (6.5%) reported currently drinking alone. In order to further explore the possibility that the respondents' alcohol use was the result of participation in friendship groups within the gay subculture, the data were examined using correlation analysis.

Participation in the Gay Subculture

As I described in chapter 4, the bar is a focal point for interaction within the gay subculture, as well as the primary setting for alcohol use. In the bar, individuals meet new friends and learn the norms of the gay world, including the social expectations related to drinking styles and etiquette. The bar, therefore, is an important context for socialization and for the formation of reference groups.

> TOM: Do you have a group of gay friends?
> JOHN: Sure.
> TOM: And how did you meet them?
> JOHN: Um, at the bars. Generally at bars, originally, and then through meeting other people. Generally, the people I know I've originally met at a bar.

For many gay men, the bar world is almost coterminous with the gay world. It would seem, therefore, that the degree of participation in the gay bar would be a good indicator of involvement in the gay world. With this in mind, the relationship between bar participation and drinking involvement was analyzed.

Reference group theory would predict that the younger a man is when he becomes involved with a group, the greater the influence it will have on him. The men were therefore asked how old they were when they first began frequenting the bars. The largest proportion of the respondents (30%) entered the bar scene between the ages of fifteen and eighteen. Another 26% began going to bars between the ages of nineteen and twenty-one, 22% were introduced to that scene between the ages of twenty-two and twenty-five, 13% entered the bar world between the ages of twenty-six and thirty, 2% became involved in the bars between the ages of thirty-one and thirty-five, and 7% of the men first went out to the bars after the age of thirty-five. The age of first regular bar attendance is negatively correlated with drinking involvement: the heavier drinkers began going to the bars at an earlier age than did the lighter alcohol users ($r = -.32$, $p<.05$). Age at first bar attendance is also correlated with frequency of bar attendance: the earlier a man began going to bars, the more frequently he was going at the time of the present study ($r = -.53$, $p<.05$). Early bar attendance is also related to whether he and his friends had chosen a particular bar as a meeting place ($r = .29$,

$p<.05$). The length of time a respondent had been going to the bar is also related to the measures of drinking involvement. The heavier drinkers had been out in the bar scene longer ($r = .29$, $p<.05$); this is also true for the problem drinkers ($r = .28$, $p<.05$).

Another variable that indicates immersion in the gay subculture is the frequency of bar attendance: the men were frequent bar-goers. As a group, they were more likely to be bar habitués than were single heterosexuals (Cosper et al., 1987; Fisher, 1981; Kraft, 1981). Sixty-five percent of my respondents went to gay bars at least once a week (22% went three to four times a week; 11% went five or six times a week; and 4% went daily), 9% attended one to three times a month, 26% went less than once a month, and no one in the sample was a nonattender. Frequency of bar attendance is correlated with alcohol consumption; the heavier drinkers were in the bar more often than were the lighter drinkers ($r = .36$, $p<.05$).

The importance of the bar as a social institution as well as a drinking context is indicated by the presence of a clique of regulars who have selected it for use as a meeting place or home territory bar. Prus (1983) notes that "one of the central elements affecting one's drinking behavior in a bar is fitting in and feeling comfortable with the other people in the setting. People entering in groups are apt to be less concerned about fitting in with other patrons and the staff" (p. 465). These cliques of regulars form a reference group, and membership in such a group is a strong indicator of socialization to the bar scene. Cosper et al. (1987) found that 35% of the Canadian tavern-users had a place they regularly attended, but that fewer than one-third of these "regulars" went to a drinking place as often as once a week. Forty-six percent of the gay men said that they and their friends used a particular bar as a base of operations.

> TOM: Are there any bars that you and your friends regularly use as a meeting place?

> MICHAEL: Satan's and the Pacific Coast. I think that's going to switch over to Gunsmoke, from what my friends tell me. It seems like a mass migration. . . . And a couple of us have talked . . . about throwing a birthday party there. . . . But [we may move to] the Golden Gate because [the owner] is a personal friend of mine. [It's] a fairly new bar and we want to start frequenting it more and we've been meaning to, but we just don't seem to get there that often.

KEVIN: Well, just [the Dungeon] I guess. I lived with some good friends when I first came here who went there a lot, and it was new; and we just got into the habit of going a lot. . . . And the other thing, too, was the drinks. You get twice the drink there . . . if you're a regular. . . . That's just the way they run their bar; they make the drinks good for the regulars and the people who tip them.

ALAN: The Pacific Coast. Everyone usually meets there. [I chose it] because of working there and knowing the employees and most of the customers.

Whether a respondent and his friends had a favorite home territory bar was correlated with alcohol consumption; the heavier drinkers were more likely to have a bar that they regularly used as a meeting place ($r = -.43$, $p<.05$).[11] Having a home territory bar was related to how frequently a respondent went to bars: the more frequently he attended, the more likely he was to have a special hangout with his friends ($r = -.44$, $p<.05$). The alcohol consumption of one's friends was also related to having a home territory bar: those men whose friends drank "a lot" were more likely to meet them in a favorite drinking establishment ($r = .28$, $p<.05$).

Finally, the relationship between the respondents' alcohol involvement and that of their friends was examined. This question gets at the very core of reference group theory, since it most directly explores the relationship between the drinking of a friendship group and an individual's own consumption (see table 6). One's consumption and that of one's friends is likely to be similar. For example, George, who was a heavy drinker on the modified Quantity-Frequency Index and a researcher-identified problem drinker, answered the question as follows.

TOM: Do your friends drink a lot or not?
GEORGE: Yes, they do [drink a lot].
TOM: And would you say you drink more than they do, about the same, or less?
GEORGE: About the same.

Forty-one percent of the men said their friends drank a lot, 50% said their friends were not excessive drinkers, and 9% said some friends were heavy drinkers while others were not. When the re-

Table 6.   Summary of Correlations Between Measures of Drinking Involvement and Measures of Participation in Gay Reference Group

| Reference Group Participation | Drinking Involvement | |
	Quanfreq	Probdrnk
1. Age at first bar attendance	−.32[a]	−.17
2. Length of time out to the bars	.29[a]	.28[a]
3. Frequency of bar attendance	.36[a]	.19
4. Favorite home territory bar	−.43[a]	−.17
5. Friends drink a lot	−.40[a]	−.45[a]

[a]$p<.05$.

spondents' perceptions of their friends' drinking is correlated with the two measures of drinking involvement, there is a significant relationship: heavier drinkers are more likely than lighter drinkers to say that their friends drank a lot ($r = -.40$, $p<.05$) and so are problem drinkers ($r = -.45$, $p<.05$).[12]

Reference group theory appears to be the most likely explanation for gay drinking: people drink because their friends drink, and they regulate their drinking in terms of the usually unstated norms of their group. In this regard, they are not different from their heterosexual peers. As Prus (1983) points out: "Drinking behavior is a social activity and can best be seen as an ongoing set of adjustments by the participants to one another. . . . The extent to which most people on most occasions consume alcohol reflects the contributions of others" (pp. 463, 474). The main difference between my respondents and the heterosexuals studied by others (e.g., Cosper et al., 1987; Fisher, 1981) is that they visit drinking establishments much more often because their social lives and sources of support are found there. Gay men have fewer alternatives than do heterosexuals.

10. Controlling Alcohol Abuse in the Gay Community

Gay Drinking in Perspective

The objective of the present study was to understand gay male drinking in a broader social context than previous work that had focused on limited aspects of the gay world such as the bar scene. The meanings embedded in alcohol use for gay men were examined, and the role drinking plays within the gay male subculture was described. Additionally, in order to understand the impact of the gay male subculture on drinking, wherever possible comparisons were made with the literature on drinking among heterosexuals.

The framework for analysis has been symbolic interaction; emphasis has been placed on drinking as social behavior, and the influence of social context (e.g., expectations in bars and the roles played by extended families and love relationships) on individual drinking patterns has been examined. By using this approach, attention has been directed to the perspective of the drinkers themselves and, accordingly, to the meanings these men place on their own and others' drinking behavior.

Many writers have identified two major factors that affect gay drinking: alienation (both alienation from others and from self) and a social world with few alternatives that are not alcohol-related (Beaton & Guild, 1976; Fifield, 1975; Lohrenz et al., 1978; Mongeon & Ziebold, 1982; Nardi, 1982a, 1982b; Small & Leach, 1977; Smith, 1982; Warren, 1974; Ziebold & Mongeon, 1982). As I argued in chapter 9,

147

alienation does not appear to account for the alcohol use of most gay men, but it is related to the consumption of problem drinkers. Alienation is a result, rather than a cause, of pathological drinking.

Alcoholic beverages are widely used by gay men because of their perception that drinking is expected in social situations. Drinking was a social activity for almost all of the men in this study. The alcohol consumption of the respondents was clearly a response to that of their friends. Their increases and decreases in drinking were strongly influenced by the drinking patterns of others. Alcohol was generally viewed very positively by the men, but even those who at first disliked the taste of alcohol or the feelings they got when drinking continued to drink because of felt social pressures.

Having problems with alcohol was not unusual for these gay men. The vast majority of them said there had been times when they had had too much to drink, and all but six men said they had worried, at one time or another, that they had been drinking too much as a lifestyle. Three-quarters of the men said they thought they might have some problems with alcohol. It was unusual, however, for them to do much about their alcohol problems.

A number of men in this study were or had been involved in long-term love relationships. While love relationships appear to reduce bar attendance, they do not necessarily affect alcohol consumption. Drinking is encouraged through participation in a closed circle of coupled associates, through adoption of an "elegant" lifestyle, and through involvement with an older, more sophisticated lover or a partner who is a bartender. In addition, the stresses and strains in a relationship, often the result of unclear role definitions and consequent power and equality issues, can increase drinking. Reductions in alcohol use, when they did occur, were often the result of feeling secure in the relationship. Drinking, which is often encouraged or at least not discouraged in the gay subculture, may lead to the dissolution of a couple.

One important finding of this study was the lack of support for sobriety among those close to my respondents. Men rarely confronted their friends about excessive drinking, nor did they support them when they had dried out. The men reported having received little positive feedback from peers during their periods of abstinence. Additionally, social supports for the men's drinking-related problems and for their attempts to deal with them were generally lacking.

Gay Drinking as a Special Situation

In most respects, gay alcoholics are little different from their heterosexual counterparts. These heavy drinkers manipulate others close to them, drink constantly at all hours, isolate themselves, cache money in secret places for drinking, run up credit card bills, become increasingly depressive, and resist labeling themselves as alcoholics. They also develop identical rationales for drinking: financial problems, difficulties on the job, and negative reactions from significant others. The gay bar world is similar to the swinging singles bar scene participated in by some heterosexuals in their twenties and early thirties, except that the gay participants span a much wider age range. Not surprisingly, Cahalan (1987), reporting on his own research on the general population, notes that "the highest proportions of heavier drinkers in both surveys were found among men in their twenties and thirties—which is consistent with findings of all known national surveys" (p. 10).

Although there are many similarities between alcohol use by heterosexual and gay drinkers, there are also important differences that make gay drinking problematic. For example, heterosexuals have numerous settings in which to meet and socialize, while gay social life is often limited to alcohol-related settings. Full participation in gay social life in American society means that one is surrounded by alcohol. Gay social life revolves around drinking because both historically and currently, homosexuals have been confined to bars for socializing. According to Smith (1982), "In most parts of the country, bars continue to be a major, if not the only, place for gay males to socialize" (p. 57). While this is changing, and there are more places where gay people can meet one another, such as churches and clubs, the bar is still the social focus of the gay world. As I have shown, the social life of the men in this study was centered around gay bar interaction, which is much more intense than comparable socializing in heterosexual bars. Some of the research reviewed in the previous chapter indicates that gays are more frequent visitors to bars. Higher percentages of gays are weekly bar attenders; conversely, significant proportions of heterosexuals do not go out to bars. Moreover, when nongays do visit drinking establishments, they often do not use alcohol (Cosper, et al., 1987; Fisher, 1981). Within the gay bar scene, there are numerous pressures to consume alcoholic beverages, including special inducements developed by the establishments themselves such as keggers and special theme nights. Bartenders also exert a subtle pressure on patrons to drink, and the social expectation is that alcohol will be consumed in these situations.

Factors Involved in Gay Problem Drinking

Based on the current study and the theoretical contributions of other researchers, a model of the acquisition of drinking problems among gays can be developed. Most men start using alcohol before they come out into the gay world, usually in their mid-teens to late teens. At this point, the majority of these young men may simply be doing what many teenagers do, and their drinking probably has no relationship to their homosexuality. For example, a household survey taken by the National Institute on Drug Abuse (1986) found that 57% of youths twelve to seventeen reported having used alcohol, and 32% said that they had done so during the previous month. For other teenagers, however, beginning to use alcohol may coincide with their first suspicions that they may be homosexual, which often occurs around the same time (Weinberg, 1983). Alcohol use, for some adolescents, is a way of allaying their fears, cultivating a masculine identity, or even rejecting the possibility that they are gay. Certainly, many of these men feel different, alone, and isolated (Colcher, 1982; Weinberg, 1983). When they do come to terms with their sexual identities, they may become estranged from their families and heterosexual friends either because they have been rejected when their sexual orientation becomes known or because they fear such rejection. Another reason for distancing themselves from family and friends is simply the greater attraction, novelty, and excitement of the gay world. When they enter the gay subculture, they are most likely to do so through the bar scene, which is the most visible gay institution. With social distance from members of the heterosexual society comes a need for alternatives, and these are developed by cultivating an extended family of other gay people (Nardi, 1982a). Having few options at first for finding a supportive group, they use the bar as a place to meet others, not only for sex but also for friendships (Diamond-Friedman, 1990). Often, they begin to organize their lives around the bars. Alcohol becomes equated with parties, fun, and social acceptance. Their peers encourage drinking, or at least do not discourage it, and they do not usually support abstinence. Some men, as I have noted, are able to drink socially and to control their alcohol intake with few, if any, problems. Others, however, develop serious drinking problems with consequent withdrawal from gay society and feelings of depression and alienation. There are also, of course, some men whose problems with alcohol predate their involvement in the gay scene. Entering the gay subculture, however, certainly seems to exacerbate their difficulties.

If a man leaves the bars, he may also find that he no longer has a social life, so there is an implicit pressure to remain involved in drinking-related settings. Those who leave the bars because they become involved in love relationships are likely to become active in a private social circle that involves home drinking. Even men whose social lives revolve around gay centers and organizations still take part in drinking, although their alcohol consumption is generally less than nonmembers of organizations. People tend to have similar ideas and hold compatible values to those of their friends, and this is reflected in their alcohol use: in general, they drink the way their friends do. Figure 1 (see p. 152) illustrates the interconnections among a variety of factors uncovered through correlation analysis.[1] It identifies a number of possible intervention points for preventing or reducing heavy and/or problem drinking within the gay male community.

Clearly, coming out at an early age is linked with problem drinking, and it is also connected to early and frequent bar attendance and the development of a favorite home territory bar. All of these factors are interconnected, as well as being linked secondarily to early alcohol use and having friends who drink heavily. This has implications for intervention. For example, since young men first coming out gravitate to the bar, other settings such as gay and lesbian youth centers offering information, activities, and the opportunity to deal with identity issues and meet others are critical in deflecting gay teens from embarking upon a career of heavy drinking. Ruefli et al. (1992a) found that organization members have significantly lower levels of bar going than do men who are not members of gay organizations.

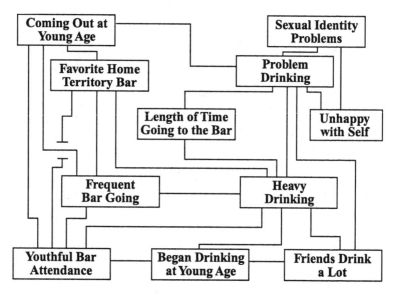

Figure 1. A processual model of gay problem drinking

Specific Strategies for Reducing Gay Problem Drinking

Reducing drinking problems in the gay community requires a strategy that is both preventative and rehabilitative and that is directed at several levels—the individual, the gay subculture, and the larger society. Mongeon and Ziebold (1982) believe that an effective approach must include "(1) improving the coping skills and competencies of individuals, (2) attempting to influence the norms of the [gay] community by providing alternate outlets for recreation and socialization, and (3) heightening the [gay] community['s] consciousness and sense of responsibility around the destructive use of alcohol by its members" (p. 92). Additionally, the place of alcohol in the larger society must be dealt with, because societal attitudes toward alcohol use affect gays as well as heterosexuals. Clearly, the alcohol use of many of the men in the present study began prior to their immersion in the gay world. In the following sections, I discuss approaches to dealing with problem drinking within the gay subculture as well as identifying some of the special needs of gay drinkers.

Prevention: Influencing Community Norms

The importance of alcohol among gay people is partly a reflection of its place in American society in general. In order for alcohol abuse to be addressed in the gay world, it must be concurrently deglamorized in the larger society. Once alcohol is no longer equated with adult status, attractiveness, sexiness, and sophistication, we should expect people to use it less. This seems to have happened with cigarettes (Goode, 1989), and a reduction in the consumption of alcohol already appears to be under way. In a survey of recent research on drinking by both the Gallup Poll and the National Institute on Drug Abuse, Goode (1989) reports that "there has been a noticeable decline in self-reported alcohol consumption between 1979 and 1985 for all ages" (p. 124). Similarly, Cahalan (1987) also reports a slight drop in alcohol consumption in the early 1980s.

What is really at issue here is the perception held by gay men that alcohol is indispensible for having a good time. Throughout this book, I have quoted men who claimed that drinking made them feel attractive and like the life of the party. Some men equate alcohol with sophistication and an upper- or upper-middle-class lifestyle. They use alcohol as a way of making claims about their own good taste and knowledge of "the finer things in life." Altering this attitude is critical in reducing the level of problem drinking and drinking-related problems.

Within the gay community itself, alternative outlets for socializing need to be developed. While gay organizations such as churches, community centers, clubs, and special interest groups do exist and certainly have multiplied since the AIDS crisis, there are not nearly enough of them to serve as alcohol-free situations for the majority of gay men. The importance of gay organizations lies in the provision of nondrinking reference groups. They are not merely other places to go to spend time that would otherwise be passed in bars. They are places where men can discover others with common interests and develop a sense of belonging and commitment. Becoming involved in gay organizations, and thus becoming integrated into a friendship network, is a process that insulates one from problem drinking. Organization members go to bars less frequently ($r = .38$, $p<.05$), do not use bars as meeting places ($r = -.30$, $p<.05$), and do not have friends who are heavy drinkers ($r = -.31$, $p<.05$).

However, since the bars are still the most important social gathering places, one logical strategy may be to provide alternatives to alcohol within the bar setting, such as a separate space where only nonalcoholic beverages are served, or hours during which only nonalcoholic drinks are available, which would alter the bar "mood" at certain times (Mongeon & Ziebold, 1982). Mongeon and Ziebold believe this makes sense because "it may be easier to alter people's drinking habits within the setting of the gay bar than to attract them to another activity altogether" (p. 97). Smith and Schneider (1981) would "encourage gay bars to make it comfortable for recover[ing] alcoholics to frequent their establishment and to limit the sale of alcohol to those gays who have a serious problem with alcohol" (p. 140). This is important because recovering gay alcoholics do frequent the bars. In the present study, five of the six recovering alcoholics continued going to bars. None of these respondents felt that bar attendance with AA friends jeopardized his sobriety. As one man said, "I stop in [the bars] after an AA meeting, or . . . a friend and I go to have a cup of coffee, say once or twice a week" (Chris).

Another alternative is to develop barlike settings in which nonalcoholic beverages are served. This is not a new idea. Some cities have had "juice bars" for many years, in both the gay and the larger communities. In one northeastern city, for instance, there is a tavern frequented by members of various AA groups in which only soft drinks, juices, and the like are served. Additionally, a recent contest took place in that city in which bartenders from establishments throughout the area attempted to make the most palatable and attractive pseudoalcoholic drink. During the time that I was in the field in Paradise City, a nonalcoholic bar for those under the age of twenty-one was established. It did not last very long, though, and was not viewed as a viable alternative by older gay men.

Developing Support Networks

As my respondents have indicated, there are few supports for sobriety within the gay community. The lack of established support structures, according to Lohrenz et al. (1978), contributes to a considerably higher rate of alcoholism among gays. In order to remedy this situation, Mongeon and Ziebold (1982) suggest that as part of a comprehensive alcohol abuse prevention program, the gay community itself can develop community education and outreach campaigns. Smith and Schneider (1981) call for more recovering gay alcoholics to become active in intervention, sponsorship, and the formation of recovery groups. Additionally, "gatekeepers" within the community such as bartenders, gym attendants, bath employees, and bookstore clerks can be trained in alcohol awareness sessions to "recognize individuals whose behavior, conversation or demeanor indicate some present difficulty with beverage alcohol" and to "intervene constructively, perhaps by suggesting some nonthreatening avenues for help" (Mongeon & Ziebold, 1982, p. 97). These well-known members of the community might also "use their influence as role models to set examples" (p. 97). Similar suggestions are made by Smith and Schneider (1981), who advocate that gay community centers, churches, bars, and free clinics be encouraged to recognize and intervene with persons having alcohol problems.

Rehabilitation: Understanding the Gay Alcoholic

There is a growing body of literature on therapeutic intervention with gay problem drinkers and alcoholics. Some of this literature describes work in hospital inpatient settings (Colcher, 1982; Smith & Schneider, 1981), while other writers examine programs established in outpatient clinics (Beaton & Guild, 1976; Driscoll, 1982) or report on work with clients or patients in private practice (Small & Leach, 1977). Other articles more generally describe the special needs of gay problem drinkers and set forth treatment strategies (Icard & Traunstein, 1987; Mongeon & Ziebold, 1982; Smith, 1982; Whitney, 1982; Zigrang, 1982). These writers deal with issues that focus on the unique nature of homosexual alcoholics and the most effective ways of working with them.

The special problems of gay alcoholics. The literature on counseling gay problem drinkers points out the special circumstances in which these individuals find themselves. Being stigmatized is a significant problem. While all alcoholics, regardless of their sexual orientation, become stigmatized if their drinking problems are known (see Trice & Roman, 1970), Smith and Schneider (1981) consider gay problem drinkers to be a doubly stigmatized minority. That is, "not only do they carry the burden of being chemically dependent [but] they [also] have to face the negative attitudes, criticism, and punitiveness from the straight community as well" (p. 131). This may cause gays to be more reluctant than heterosexuals to seek help for their drinking problems. Gay people tend to be hesitant to reveal themselves to heterosexual therapists for fear of rejection and are therefore underrepresented in patient populations (Colcher, 1982; Driscoll, 1982; Smith, 1982; Smith & Schneider, 1981; Zigrang, 1982). Thus, there is some debate on the appropriateness or effectiveness of having heterosexuals work with gays (e.g., Driscoll, 1982; Mongeon & Ziebold, 1982; Ziebold, 1978; Zigrang, 1982).

A number of writers (Icard & Traunstein, 1987; Small & Leach, 1977; Smith, 1982; Smith & Schneider, 1981) claim that gay problem drinkers have ambivalent feelings about their sexuality, problems of self-acceptance, and low self-esteem. I have reported similar problems among the alcoholics in the present study. Gay alcoholics may emphasize their sexual orientation to the point of feeling that they cannot relate to the concerns or lifestyles of heterosexual problem drinkers (Beaton & Guild, 1976; Smith & Schneider, 1981).[2] Individual gay people and the gay community itself tend to be isolated from the majority community (Beaton & Guild, 1976; Smith & Schneider, 1981), leaving few opportunities to socialize that are not alcohol-related (Beaton & Guild, 1976; Icard & Traunstein, 1987). This was also a common theme expressed by the respondents in the present study. Youth and physical appearance are strongly stressed in the gay community, probably to a more extreme degree than among heterosexuals (Beaton & Guild, 1976). Smith (1982) notes that self-esteem is frequently a problem for all alcoholics but that for gay men it is often highly related to body image. Body image, he writes, is often linked with problems in sexual functioning, which may in turn result in heavy drinking. The gay male alcoholic, seeing his body "prematurely aging," may believe the myth "that life after forty will indeed be bleak" (p. 66).

Working with the gay problem drinker. Several writers have proposed strategies for working with the individual gay problem drinker that take into account his special situation. For example, stigma can be reduced by developing counseling situations that are warm and supportive, a "safe milieu" (Smith & Schneider, 1981). This requires special education and training programs to sensitize counselors to the situation of gay clients (Colcher, 1982; Zigrang, 1982). Stigma can also be reduced by concentrating on the problem of alcoholism rather than on the individual's homosexuality (Beaton & Guild, 1976; Colcher, 1982; Small & Leach, 1977). Smith (1982) recommends using a "bifocal approach," in which the therapist focuses on the alcoholism as he or she would with any client, while simultaneously also keeping the individual's special situation as a gay alcoholic in mind. In order to do this, the therapist must be familiar with the life stages of gay men and the way in which these stages affect and are affected by their alcoholism.

Problems of self-acceptance, low self-esteem, and ambivalence about one's sexual orientation can be dealt with by encouraging "a change from a passive, victim-restrictive stance to an active, creator-constructive stance" (Smith, 1982, p. 54). Beaton and Guild (1976) report that "group leaders thought it important to refute the premise that to be gay and alcoholic meant that group members had to remain helpless victims of their own dependencies and of society's prejudice" (p. 307). Coming to terms with one's homosexuality is related to accepting one's alcoholism (Small & Leach, 1977). These problems may also be helped by the acceptance most gays receive when they reveal themselves in heterosexual alcohol therapy groups (Smith & Schneider, 1981; Zigrang, 1982). Identifying gay counselors in these programs who may serve as positive role models has also been seen as a positive influence, both for accepting oneself and for becoming comfortable within a therapy situation (Smith & Schneider, 1981; Zigrang, 1982). The integration of alcoholism experts within gay community center programs and the use of Gay AA as an adjunct to individual or group therapy have also been suggested (Colcher, 1982).

In sum, the literature on working with gay alcoholics stresses that their alcoholism should be the primary concern, while advising counselors to be familiar with gay lifestyles so that the special needs of gay clients can be served. Smith (1982), in particular, emphasizes that one should take a phenomenological view of gay drinking by attempting to understand how the individual sees himself, his world, and the part his drinking plays in his life.

Finally, members of extended families must become alcohol-aware and support sobriety. Significant others rarely confront problem drinkers about their alcohol use, and they usually do not encourage them during abstinent periods. Sometimes, these significant others such as lovers, friends, and extended family members become enablers or co-alcoholics, "person[s] in the alcoholic's life who intervene in such a way as to prevent the alcoholic from facing the consequences of his action" (Whitney, 1982, p. 37). Whitney emphasizes that "if treatment personnel are to adopt a whole-system inter-vention when working with the gay male alcoholic, they must begin to look very closely at the social support system that has maintained the addiction" (p. 38). Working with co-alcoholics and making them aware of the issues underlying their own behavior is critical in help-ing their friends and lovers who have drinking problems.

Appendix:
Interview
Schedule

This is a study in which we are interested in the attitudes of gay men toward alcoholic beverages and their experience with alcohol. You have been included in the sample because you are a gay man living in the Paradise City area. I'd like to ask you about your use of alcoholic beverages and your feelings about them.

1. First of all, about how frequently do you use alcohol?
2. What alcoholic beverages do you usually drink?
3. About how many drinks do you usually have when you are drinking?
4. In what situations do you usually use alcohol?
5. Are there certain situations in which you drink more or less than usual?
6. Do you usually drink alone or with other people?
7. Do you ever drink alone? (Probe circumstances.)
8. How old were you when you first began drinking in a fairly consistent way?
9. How did this occur? (Probe where, with whom, under what circumstances, etc.)
10. How did you feel about it?
11. What sorts of beverages were you drinking then?
12. How much were you drinking?
13. Do you go to gay bars? (If respondent does not go, ask, Have you ever gone? Why don't you go anymore? If respondent has never attended gay bars, ask, Why haven't you gone to gay bars? Do you think you'll ever go in the future? Under what circumstances might you go?)

Skip to question 50 if respondent has never gone to gay bars.

14. How old were you when you first began going to gay bars?
15. Where was this?
16. Did you first "come out" in the bar scene? (If respondent answers yes, say, Tell me about it.)

161

17. What did you drink at first? How much did you drink? How frequently?
18. What do you usually drink now when you go to bars? How much?
19. Has your drinking style changed since you first started going to the bars? (If respondent says yes, ask, In what ways? Probe further in terms of type of beverage, amount used, drinking partners, settings, feelings, and behavior when drinking. Ask, How do you account for this change or these changes?)
20. Which bars do you go to?
21. Has this changed over the years? (If yes, ask, Why have you changed bars?)
22. How often do you go out to the bars?
23. Is this more or less than you have gone in the past? (If different, ask, How do you account for this change?)
24. Do you usually go to the bars alone or with other people?
25. Has this changed over time? (If yes, ask, What do you think accounts for this change?)
26. Is going to the bars alone (or with others) a preference you have? (Ask, What do you think accounts for your going to the bars [either alone or with others]?)

Skip to question 28 if respondent goes out to bars with others.

27. Do you generally have plans to join a group of other people there? (If respondent answers no, ask, Do you usually have plans to join one other person there?)
28. Are there any bars that you and your friends regularly use as a meeting place? (If respondent answers yes, ask, Which ones? How did you come to choose this [these] bar[s] rather than some others?)
29. What makes a particular bar appealing to you? (Probe: good music, the type of people who go there, attitudes of owners, bartenders, etc.)
30. What do you feel are your own needs that the bars help to fill? (Probe: meeting people as sexual partners or social friends, to dance, to drink, just to have something to do, etc.)
31. Over the years, what are some of the reasons you have had for going to the bars?
32. Are there times during which you go just to drink and other times when you go to have a good time or to meet sexual partners? (Ask, Has this changed over time?)

Skip to question 34 if respondent answers no to question 32.

33. How does going to the bar for (insert respondent's reason) affect what and how much you drink? (Probe each reason mentioned.)
34. Do you usually visit more than one bar when you go out? (If yes, ask,

How many bars do you usually go to? Which bars are these?) (If no, ask, Do you ever go to more than one bar in an evening?)

If respondent answers no, skip to question 40.

35. If respondent answers yes to question 34 or the probe, ask, If you do go to more than one bar when you are going out, do you do this every time you go to the bars or just sometimes?
36. Under what circumstances do you usually go to more than one bar when you go out?
37. Under what circumstances do you remain at the first bar you go to? (Probe the relationship between the respondent's original motivation for going to the bar and his bar-visiting behavior.)
38. Do your original reasons for going to the bar sometimes change while you are there? (If yes, ask, How does this affect your drinking?)
39. When you go to more than one bar, do you do this alone or with other people? Why?
40. Do you have a particular routine you follow every time you go to the bars? (If respondent says yes, say, Tell me about it.)
41. Do you ever go to the bars during the day? (If respondent says yes, ask, Which bars are these? Under what circumstances would you go during the day?)
42. Do you drink at every bar you visit?
43. Do you drink alcoholic beverages every time you go out?
44. Do you drink more at some bars than others? (If respondent says yes, ask, What accounts for this? Does what you drink vary with the particular bar you are in at the time?)

If respondent answers no to question 44, skip to question 46.

45. In what way does your drinking vary? What do you think accounts for this?
46. What determines for you how long you stay in a particular bar?
47. Do you usually stay about the same length of time in a particular bar every time you go there? (If yes, ask, About how long is this?)
48. About how much of what kind of drinks would you have during a usual evening at the bars?
49. Describe for me your typical night at the bar.
50. Do you ever go to straight bars? (If respondent answers yes, probe frequency, circumstances, etc.)
51. In what settings would you say most of your drinking takes place? (Probe: bars, beaches, own home, homes of others, private parties, parks, other public settings, straight bars or settings.)
52. Is there any specific reason for this?

53. Tell me about the other settings in which you also drink. (Be certain to probe each setting mentioned in question 51, including frequency, reasons for attending, whether respondent goes with others or alone, etc.)

54. Do you have a group of gay friends?

If respondent answers no, skip to question 59.

55. How did you meet them? (Ask, In what settings do you usually meet other gay people?)

56. Do you drink more or less on these occasions than you do at the bars or in some public setting?

57. Do your friends drink a lot or not?

58. Do you drink more, the same, or less than they do?

59. What are some of the reasons you have for drinking?

60. Do your reasons for drinking vary with the situation? (Ask, In what ways?)

61. How do you usually feel when you have been drinking?

62. Does this vary with the situation and the amount you've had to drink? (Ask, In what way?)

63. Have there ever been any periods or times during which you did not drink for a while? (If respondent says yes, say, Tell me about them. Probe circumstances, respondent's feelings, why he stopped drinking, and why he resumed using alcohol.)

If respondent answers no to question 63, skip to question 65.

64. How did others around you respond to your stopping drinking?

65. Are there any times when you feel like you've had too much to drink?

If respondent answers no to question 65, skip to question 67.

66. What are those times like? (Ask, How often does this happen? What has been going on in your life during those times?)

67. Have you ever thought you might have some problems with alcohol? (If respondent says yes, probe reasons for his answer.)

If respondent answers no to question 67, skip to question 69.

68. What have you done about it?

69. Have you ever worried that you may have been drinking too much?

If respondent answers no to question 69, skip to question 71.

70. What did you do about it?
71. Have you ever had any problems as a result of your drinking? (If respondent answers yes, ask, Of what sort? Probe: fights, ejection from bars, loss of friends or family, alienation from lovers, loss of job, disciplinary action at school, trouble with the law, arrests, accidents, etc.)

If respondent says no to question 71, skip to question 78.

72. Tell me about it. (Probe: how problem occurred, what happened afterward, feelings of respondent. Did problem occur while he was actually drinking or drunk? Was he involved in any relationships at the time? Was this related?)
73. How did others around you respond to these problems? (Probe for reactions of family, friends, lovers, etc.)
74. How did you feel about their responses?
75. What did you do about these problems? (Probe: Did respondent discontinue drinking or going to particular drinking-related places, seek counseling, go to AA, etc.?)
76. How did others around you respond to what you did about your drinking-related problems?
77. How did you feel about their responses?
78. Have your friends ever told you that you've had too much to drink?

If respondent says no to question 78, skip to question 80.

79. What did they do about it? How did you feel about what they did?
80. Have your friends ever told you that they thought you had a drinking problem?

If respondent says no to question 80, skip to question 84.

81. What were their reasons for saying this?
82. How did you feel about this?
83. What did they do about it? (Ask, Did they try to help you?)
84. Have you ever told friends they had a drinking problem?

If respondent says no to question 84, skip to question 89.

85. Why did you do this?
86. How did they respond to what you told them?
87. How did you feel about their response?
88. What did you do about it?
89. Are you involved in a long-term love relationship now? (If respondent says yes, ask, Are you living with your lover?)

90. If respondent says no to question 89, ask, Have you ever been in a long-term love relationship in the past?

If respondent says no to questions 89 and 90, skip to question 95.

91. How do your love relationships affect your drinking? (Probe: amount, frequency, time spent in various drinking-related settings, etc.)
92. Do you drink more or less when you are involved in a relationship with someone?
93. Does this affect your going to bars? (Ask, In what ways?)
94. How does (did) your lover (lovers) feel about your drinking?
95. How many really close friends do you have in the (Paradise City) area?
96. Whom do you usually talk to about your most intimate feelings?
97. If something very significant happened in your life, how many people are there in the (Paradise City) area with whom you could share this?
98. Who are these people and what are their relationships to you?
99. Have you ever felt that you were alone, without anyone to whom you could turn?

If respondent says no to question 99, skip to question 101.

100. Tell me about it. (Ask, When was this? What were the circumstances? Where were you living at the time? What did you do about it, etc.?)

I want to thank you for answering these questions. Now, I have a few background questions to ask.

101. What is your date of birth?
102. Where were you born?
103. Where did you grow up?
104. If respondent did not grow up in (Paradise City) area, ask, How long have you been living in the (Paradise City) area?
105. Where does your family live? (If family is not living in the area, ask, Do you have relatives living here?)
106. How often do you have contact with members of your family?
107. How close do you feel toward your parents (brothers, sisters, etc.)? (Ask, With whom in your family are you especially close?)
108. What is your occupation? (Alternative wording: What do you do for a living?)
109. What are the occupations of your parents?
110. How many years of schooling have you completed?
111. How many years of schooling have your parents completed?
112. Do your parents use alcohol? (If respondent answers yes, ask, Have they had any problems with it?)

113. Have your brothers or sisters had problems with drinking?
114. What is your religious background?
115. Do you still practice this religion or any other? (If a different religion from original, ask which one.)
116. If respondent practices a religion, ask, How strongly are you committed to it?
117. What is your nationality/ethnic background?
118. What is your approximate yearly income?
119. What area of Paradise City are you living in now?
120. With whom are you living?
121. Do you know your neighbors? (If respondent says yes, ask, Are you friendly with them?)
122. Are your neighbors aware that you are gay? (If respondent says yes, ask, How do they seem to feel about it?)
123. Does your family know about your sexual orientation? (If respondent says yes, ask, How do they feel about it? How do you feel about this?)
124. Who else knows about your being gay?
125. How old were you when you first decided that you were definitely gay (and knew what that meant)?
126. How long ago was this?
127. How did you feel about it?
128. What did you do about your feelings?
129. How do you feel about being gay now?
130. How happy are you with yourself as a person?
131. How happy are you with your life?
132. Do you ever get depressed? (If respondent says yes, ask, When does this happen? What do you usually do about it?)
133. Do you belong to any gay or homophile organizations? (If respondents says yes, ask, Which ones?)
134. How active are you in these organizations? (Probe: offices held, frequency of attendance at meetings, and so forth.)

These are all of the prepared questions I have. Is there anything that we have missed or that we didn't cover thoroughly enough that you can think of? Is there something else you would like to add?

Notes

1. Gay Men and Drinking: An Introduction

1. Fifield (1975) defined "an alcoholic or one who abuses alcohol to 'problem drinker' proportions" as "a person who repeatedly drinks to excess and may or may not cause behavioral disturbances" (p. 45). It is not clear, however, what Fifield means by "excess." Additionally, her methodology has severe flaws. Her survey was broad-based, and included bar owners and bartenders; members of Alcoholics Together, an organization for gays modeled after AA; participants in Van Ness Recovery House, a state licensed facility for men located in the Los Angeles "gay ghetto"; lesbians from the Alcoholism Program for Women; and staff members of various social agencies. But the core of her data was based on the self-reports of bar patrons. She projected these reports onto what she estimated to be the total gay population of Los Angeles County, arriving at an estimate that 32% of the county's gays were alcohol abusers or problem drinkers. The Fifield project is notable for its scope and the ambition with which it was undertaken, yet it is marred by a number of serious methodological errors. For example, 100 of approximately 300 gay bars, compiled from a number of sources such as gay bar guides and travel books, were selected by using a table of random numbers. Then, one bartender and two bar patron questionnaires were distributed to each bar. However, the attempt at probability sampling breaks down here, since respondents in each bar were not randomly selected. In addition, where resistance to filling out questionnaires was encountered, or where a bar was no longer in existence, substitution was allowed, thus destroying any pretense of "scientific" sample selection (Fifield, 1975, p. 25). Fifield admitted that the bartenders' estimates of the percentages of problem drinkers were unreliable. In her words, "many bartenders were uncooperative and resistant to giving any estimate of the percent of their customers who are alcoholics or problem drinkers" (p. 28). Given even the most willing bartender, the accuracy of his estimate could be questioned. Fifield also used bar patrons' estimates of their drinking.

Using a series of calculations, she combined their estimates of the number of times they went to bars during a given period of time, the number of bars they visited, and the number of drinks they consumed. This information was related to estimates of the number of gay bars and gay people in Los Angeles County, which were also based on very tenuous guesses (see pp. 36–44). Her statistical measures, no matter how "scientifically" manipulated, are all based, at best, on guesswork. They are treated, however, as if they were all "real" and valid. Despite these criticisms, Fifield's work represents a very real contribution to the literature on gays and drinking. Hers is a pioneering effort notable for the ambition with which it was undertaken, the variety of data gathered, and the attempt to develop a sociological theory to account for gay alcohol-related problems.

2. In Stall and Wiley (1988), men who drank five or more drinks on a single occasion and more often than once a week were labeled frequent/heavy drinkers. Men who used alcohol at least once a week, but never drank more than four drinks at a time were classified as frequent/light drinkers. Those respondents who drank less than once a week but at least once a month were infrequent drinkers, and those who drank less than once a month but at least once a year were rated as occasional drinkers. Abstainers were those men who had not used alcohol during the previous year. The Quantity-Frequency Index used in my study was modified by Engs (1977), from Straus and Bacon (1953). It combines the absolute alcohol content of various drinks with the number of drinks used over a given period of time, so that frequency is not separated from quantity as in the Stall and Wiley study.

2. Research Methods

1. Paradise City is a pseudonym. Names of areas within Paradise City, names of bars, and names of respondents have all been changed to protect their anonymity.

2. A copy of the interview schedule appears in the appendix.

3. See chapter 6 (especially table 4) for a discussion of current drinking patterns.

4. The Metropolitan Community Church, the first gay church, was established by the Reverend Troy Perry in 1968 in Los Angeles. Since that time, congregations have been established in many large cities throughout the United States.

5. See chapter 4 for a discussion of the bar scene and its geographic distribution.

3. Drinking as Social Behavior

1. This tendency for gays to have drinking habits similar to those of their friends does not differentiate them from heterosexuals. Kraft (1981), for instance, found that the heavy drinkers among the college students whom he surveyed were more likely than light or moderate drinkers to report having one or more friends with drinking problems. The present research is not exactly comparable to the Kraft study, since the men in the gay sample were somewhat older (the median age was twenty-nine). The Kraft sample did include graduate students (22%) and "others," probably nonmatriculated students, so it is likely that the median age of his students was in the early twenties. A more comparable sample of heterosexuals in terms of age is found in Aitken's (1985) study of pub behavior among young adults in Scotland. He reported that "males whose companions consumed relatively large amounts of alcohol tended to consume relatively large amounts themselves. This variable, considered alone, accounted for 62% of the variance in alcohol consumption" (p. 449).

2. Fifteen men (32.6%) reported drinking only with others, and the rest of the respondents said that they drank both in social situations and by themselves. These responses should be interpreted with caution, since they really reflect the men's perceptions of their drinking more than their actual drinking. Two men, for instance, who had previously said that they never drank alone, later indicated that they did have wine with solitary dinners or a liqueur afterwards with coffee. They felt that this did not count as "drinking alone." The drinking patterns of some men who had reported consuming alcohol with others as well as by themselves involved going to bars, but isolating themselves from interaction with other bar patrons. Sociologically, these men should more accurately be described as solitary, not social, drinkers. This pattern was typical of the alcoholics in the study.

3. This classification was made using Engs's (1977) modification of Straus and Bacon's (1953) Quantity-Frequency Index. See chapter 6 for the distribution of men in the sample by this method.

4. I do not know exactly how the respondents' drinking compared with that of their friends, since specific questions about the amount and frequency of friends' drinking were not asked. I do have some data on the men's general perceptions of the quantity of their friends' consumption. Forty-one percent of the men said their friends drank a lot, 50% said their friends did not drink a lot, and 9% said that some of their friends drank a lot, while others were moderate drinkers. Obviously, terms like *a lot*, *more*, and *less* are imprecise and subjective. Yet in an interactionist study that focuses primarily on people's perceptions, more specific definitions are neither possible nor particularly useful. Some men could give only rough guesses about their own alcohol consumption.

5. By social context, I mean those activities, scenes, and settings in which we participate, as they are defined by the people around us.

4. The Bar

1. Cosper et al. (1987) found that 30% of the nondrinkers in a national survey of 1,708 Canadians aged eighteen and over went at least occasionally to public drinking places.

2. By contrast, Cavan (1966) studied both homosexual and heterosexual bars and found that although there was some pressure in heterosexual bars to drink, the beverage did not necessarily have to be alcoholic.

3. The water referred to by Ted is bottled sparkling water such as Perrier or Calistoga, which costs, in Paradise City, about $1.00 to $1.50 a bottle, about the same price as bottled beer. In addition, most bars serve fruit juices or soft drinks.

4. This mediation on the part of bar personnel also occurred in the heterosexual cocktail lounge studied by Roebuck and Spray (1967). However, the bar personnel in the Sultan do not seem to regard the matchmaking function as one of their exclusive prerogatives, as did the bartenders and waitresses in the Roebuck and Spray study.

5. Jones et al. (1987) also found persistent patterns of high risk sexual behavior in a sample of gay men. The research was done in 1985 and examined the behavior of men in New Mexico, which at that time had a low incidence of HIV infection. One possibility is that risk taking is related to the perception of possible infection. Leigh (1990) found high rates of risky sex among heterosexuals, who see themselves as less likely to come into contact with the AIDS virus. Windle (1989) studied heterosexual alcoholic inpatients in western New York in roughly the same geographic area where Ruefli et al. (1992a, 1992b) obtained their sample of gay men, and also found risky behavior, including unprotected vaginal and anal sex, multiple partners, and IV drug use among a subset of his sample. Kelly, St. Lawrence, Brasfield, Stevenson et al. (1990) studied bar patrons in Seattle, Washington, Mobile, Alabama, and Tampa, Florida, which have low to moderate AIDS prevalence rates compared to the original AIDS epicenters. They found that 37% of their sample had engaged in high-risk sexual behavior within the preceding three months. Men who acknowledged engaging in unprotected anal intercourse underestimated their actual risk level. The relationship between risk assessment and sexual behavior is not clear, however. Emmons et al. (1986) reported "an absence of a consistent and positive relationship between perceived risk and behavioral changes" (p. 340). Joseph et al. (1987) did not find any evidence that perceiving oneself to be at an

increased risk for AIDS is related to reductions in one's high-risk behavior, and the data indicate that the opposite may be the case.

6. At a kegger, one pays a flat admission price, usually $1.00 or $2.00, and then is entitled to unlimited refills of beer throughout the evening or until a predetermined number of kegs has been consumed. Some kegger parties are free.

7. Examples of such special nights are "full moon" parties, "roller disco" night, "butch-as-a-three-dollar-bill" contests, "leatherman" night, "bare back/torn levi" night, "hat" night, and so forth, during which beer and other drinks are provided at low cost. They parallel the "wet T-shirt" contests sponsored by heterosexual singles bars.

8. What constitutes such a proper atmosphere varies widely. For some men, it means the availability of intelligent people who can carry on a pleasant conversation in a quiet setting; for others, it is a large number of "hot" (i.e., sexually attractive) men dancing to loud music with a pulsating beat, exuding what one man characterized as a "high-energy" level.

5.   Love Relationships and Drinking

1. I interviewed three pairs of lovers: Steven and Bill, Art and Ernie, and Frank and Erik, who were living together at the time they were interviewed.

2. Two years after his interview, Steven, with whom I had kept in contact, telephoned me to say that he had joined AA. He had broken up his Holy Union with Bill, and now characterized himself as having been an "elegant alcoholic," one whose heavy drinking was related to an "upper-class" style of alcohol consumption.

3. In addition, three men said that the effect of a relationship on bar attendance depended on one's partner, one man said that being in a couple had not affected his bar visits at all because he and his lover went there together, and seven men could not answer the question.

4. None of the quotations from the heterosexually married women about their husbands' drinking and their own reactions to this situation from the Weinberg and Vogler (1990) study presented in this chapter appear in the cited article. They are from data that have not been previously published.

5. The drinking age in Western State is twenty-one. In both cases, however, these men and their lovers did drink at home.

6. Three men said that the changes in their drinking depended on their partners; six others reported that their drinking was not affected.

7. Again, these quotations are from data that have not been previously published.

6.   Drinking Careers

1. The idea that one's behavior and experiences can be organized into a "career" is not the unique invention of sociologists. It is common for lay people to retrospectively attempt to understand their biographies using the notion of career as a sense-making device (Watson & Weinberg, 1982). Some of my respondents saw their histories as alcoholics in precisely this way. For example, one man explicitly used the term *career* to describe his drinking: "Most of my bars were primarily straight bars and remained so during my drinking career, when I wasn't with a lover" (Joel).

2. Lutherans Concerned and Dignity are organizations for gay Lutherans and gay Catholics, respectively.

3. Goode (1989), for example, presents data from a study by the National Institute on Drug Abuse (1986) showing that 57% of youths between the ages of twelve and seventeen reported having consumed alcohol, and that one-third had done so in the month preceding the survey. (See also pp. 134–36.) Earlier studies of drinking among young people are summarized by Maddox (1962). Ullman (1962) also presents data on the first drinking experiences of college students.

4. See, for example, Straus and Bacon (1962).

5. Only 4% of the students in Kraft's (1981) study reported having gotten a buzz on or become tipsy or high three or more times a week. Another 17% did so once or twice a week.

6. Percentages for both groups add up to over 100%, since some individuals reported more than one problem.

7. In a study reported by Driscoll (1982), based on 1,087 returned and usable questionnaires (out of 15,000 distributed through a gay organization), 19% of the respondents said that they drank daily, 22% drank three to four times a week, 28% drank mainly on weekends, 3% reported days or weeks of heavy drinking, 5% were abstainers, and 5% were former drinkers.

8.   Problem Drinkers

1. The difference between these two concepts is illustrated by a man who said, "[When I first began drinking] it was more a party thing all the time. But now it's just like a natural part of me, you know" (Chuck).

2. George, Richard, Jeffrey, P. J., John, Patrick, Kevin, Jack, Alan, Scott, and Norman were researcher-identified problem drinkers; Ted, Bruce, Chuck, and Gary were self-identified alcoholics who were still drinking; and Todd, Vinnie, Kenneth, Barry, Joel, and Chris were self-identified recovering alcoholics.

3. Jellinek's (1962) formulation has been criticized by a number of writers

(e.g., Cahalan, 1987; Little, 1989, McCaghy, 1976, Rudy, 1986) who disagree with his sequential model of alcoholism and his classification of different types of alcoholics. These critics also depreciate the support his work gives to those who hold a disease concept of alcoholism. Yet his work continues to be cited, and his observations of some of the concomitants of alcoholism such as preoccupation with alcohol and surreptitious drinking are accurate depictions of some problem drinkers.

4. In Ted's case, the interview actually facilitated the phenomenon it was designed to reveal: the interview itself became part of the data (see also Watson & Weinberg, 1982).

5. Rudy's (1986) respondents revealed similarly violent incidents (see pp. 22 and 110–11).

9. Alternative Explanations for Gay Problem Drinking

1. In his development of a theoretical explanation for gay drinking, Nardi's primary emphasis in his larger body of work is on extended families and friendship networks, rather than on alienation (see Nardi, 1982a).

2. See also Colcher's (1982) comments on the isolation of gay alcoholics (p. 47).

3. The essence of Merton's (1949) argument is that in societies in which elements of the social structure effectively block groups of individuals from obtaining access to culturally approved means of achieving culturally desired ends that are supposed to be available to all members, alienation (i.e., anomy) occurs among the disenfranchised, resulting in a variety of individual deviant adjustments. All of these adjustments involve rejecting or accepting culturally defined goals (ends) and means in a variety of combinations. For example, "innovators" reject the means and substitute alternative ("deviant") ways of achieving the society's goals.

4. As Seeman points out, his use of isolation is similar to Merton's (1949) conceptualization of rebellion, in which the individual rejects both goals and means, and wishes instead to see his own goals and means institutionalized.

5. The data were not appropriate for an analysis of all the dimensions identified by Seeman.

6. For consistency, the currently abstinent self-labeled alcoholics were scored as heavy drinkers on the modified Quantity-Frequency Index, since they were treated that way in the discussion in chapter 8, and because their nondrinking behaviors were more like those of currently drinking problem drinkers than they were like those of persons who had never been involved with alcohol in the past.

7. Goode (1989) points out that

> heavy drinkers may (and often do) become problem drinkers; problem drinkers are usually (but not necessarily) heavy drinkers. Getting

into various kinds of trouble is one possible outcome of drinking a lot, but not a necessary one. The notion of the problem drinker is sociologically useful because it is the opposite of the 'objective' definition of alcoholism . . . the consumption of 15 centiliters of absolute alcohol a day. The notion of problem drinker is based on *how people see what happens to the drinker's life, supposedly as a result of unwise or excessive drinking* [Goode's italics]. (pp. 129–30)

8. Percentages total over 100% because some respondents shared significant events with others in more than one category.

9. Percentages total over 100% because some respondents shared their intimate feelings with others in more than one category.

10. The variables run in the opposite direction because whether the respondent ever got depressed was coded 1 for yes and 2 for no.

11. The variables run in the opposite direction because whether the respondent and his friends regularly used a particular bar as a meeting place was coded 1 for yes and 2 for no.

12. The variables run in the opposite direction because whether friends drank a lot was coded 1 for yes and 2 for no.

10.   Controlling Alcohol Abuse in the Gay Community

1. Those correlations that have not been previously presented are: (1) coming out at a young age and (a) problem drinking ($r = -.26$, $p<.05$) (b) having a favorite home territory bar ($r = .26$, $p<.05$) (c) youthful bar attendance ($r = .72$, $p<.05$) and (d) frequent bar going ($r = -.43$, $p<.05$); (2) youthful bar attendance and (a) having a favorite home territory bar ($r = .29$, $p<.05$) (b) frequent bar going ($r = -.53$, $p<.05$) and (c) having begun drinking at a young age ($r = .34$, $p<.05$); (3) having begun drinking at a young age and (a) heavy drinking ($r = -.44$, $p<.05$) and (b) having friends who drink a lot ($r = .31$, $p<.05$); (4) having a favorite home territory bar and frequent bar going ($r = -.44$, $p<.05$); (5) having sexual identity problems and being unhappy with oneself ($r = .27$, $p<.05$).

2. This point was made during a Gay AA meeting I attended. A former member of the group who was back for a visit complained to the other people present that he was uncomfortable and unable to identify with the heterosexual AA group in his new city. The other people in the gay group emphasized to him that what was important was his sobriety, and that his recovery could be accomplished within a largely heterosexual setting.

References

Abraham, K. (1954). The psychological relations between sexuality and alcoholism. In E. Jones (Ed.), *Selected Papers of Karl Abraham* (pp. 80–89). New York: Basic Books. (Original work published 1908)

Achilles, N. (1967). The development of the homosexual bar as an institution. In J. H. Gagnon & W. Simon (Eds.), *Sexual deviance* (pp. 228–244). New York: Harper & Row.

Adam, B. D. (1979). A social history of gay politics. In M. P. Levine (Ed.), *Gay men: The sociology of male homosexuality* (pp. 285–300). New York: Harper & Row.

Aitken, P. P. (1985). An observational study of young adults' drinking groups: 2. Drink purchasing procedures, group pressures and alcohol consumption by companions as predictors of alcohol consumption. *Alcohol and Alcoholism, 20*, 445–457.

Barringer, F. (1993, April 15). Sex survey of American men finds 1% are gay. *New York Times*, p. A1.

Beaton, S., & Guild, N. (1976). Treatment for gay problem drinkers. *Social Casework, 57*, 302–308.

Becker, H. S. (1963). *Outsiders: Studies in the sociology of deviance.* New York: The Free Press.

Berelson, B., & Steiner, G. A. (1964). *Human behavior: An inventory of scientific findings.* New York: Harcourt.

Blum, E. M. (1966). Psychoanalytic views of alcoholism: A review. *Quarterly Journal of Studies on Alcohol, 27*, 259–299.

Botwinick, J., & Machover, S. (1951). A psychometric examination of latent homosexuality in alcoholism. *Quarterly Journal of Studies on Alcohol, 12*, 268–272.

Cahalan, D. (1970). *Problem drinkers: A national survey.* San Francisco: Jossey-Bass.

Cahalan, D. (1987). *Understanding America's drinking problem: How to combat the hazards of alcohol.* San Francisco: Jossey-Bass.

Cavan, S. (1966). *Liquor license.* Chicago: Aldine.

Charon, J. M. (1985). *Symbolic interactionism: An introduction, an interpretation, an integration* (2nd ed.). Englewood Cliffs, NJ: Prentice-Hall.

Clark, W. B. (1981). Public drinking contexts: Bars and taverns. In T. C. Harford & L. C. Gaines (Eds.), *Social drinking contexts* (Research Monograph No. 7) (pp. 8–33). Rockville, MD: National Institute on Alcohol Abuse and Alcoholism.

Cohen, A. K. (1955). *Delinquent boys: The culture of the gang.* New York: The Free Press.

Colcher, R. W. (1982). Counseling the homosexual alcoholic. *Journal of Homosexuality, 7*(4), 43–52.

Connell, R. W., & Kippax, S. (1990). Sexuality in the AIDS crisis: Patterns of sexual practice and pleasure in a sample of Australian gay and bisexual men. *Journal of Sex Research, 27,* 167–198.

Connor, R. G. (1962). The self-concepts of alcoholics. In D. J. Pittman & C. R. Snyder (Eds.), *Society, culture, and drinking patterns* (pp. 455–467). Carbondale, IL: Southern Illinois University Press.

Cosper, R. L., Okraku, I. O., & Neumann, B. (1987). Tavern going in Canada: A national survey of regulars at public drinking establishments. *Journal of Studies on Alcohol, 8,* 252–259.

Dank, B. M. (1971). Coming out in the gay world. *Psychiatry: Journal for the Study of Interpersonal Processes, 34,* 180–197.

Dean, D. G. (1961). Alienation: Its meaning and measurement. *American Sociological Review, 26,* 753–758.

Delph, E. W. (1978). *The silent community: Public homosexual encounters.* Beverly Hills, CA: Sage.

Diamond-Freidman, C. (1990). A multivariant model of alcoholism specific to gay-lesbian populations. *Alcoholism Treatment Quarterly, 7,* 111–117.

Driscoll, R. (1982). A gay-identified alcohol treatment program: A follow-up study. *Journal of Homosexuality, 7*(4), 71–80.

Durkheim, E. (1951). *Suicide: A study in sociology.* (G. Simpson, Ed., J. A. Spaulding & G. Simpson, Trans.). New York: The Free Press. (Original work published 1897)

Emmons, C-A., Joseph, J. G., Kessler, R. C., Wortman, C. B., Montgomery, S. B., & Ostrow, D. G. (1986). Psychosocial predictors of reported behavior change in homosexual men at risk for AIDS. *Health Education Quarterly, 13,* 331–345.

Engs, R. C. (1977). Drinking patterns and drinking problems of college students. *Journal of Studies on Alcohol, 38,* 2144–2156.

Fenichel, O. (1945). The psychoanalytic theory of neurosis. New York: Norton.

Fifield, L. (1975). *On my way to nowhere: Alienated, isolated, drunk; An analysis of gay alcohol abuse and an evaluation of alcoholism rehabilitation services for the Los Angeles gay community.* Los Angeles: Gay Community Services Center.

Fifield, L. H., Lathan, J. D., & Phillips, C. (1977). *Alcoholism in the gay community: The price of alienation, isolation and oppression.* Los Angeles: Gay Community Services Center.

Fisher, J. C. (1981). Psychosocial correlates of tavern use: A national probability sample study. In T. C. Harford & L. S. Gaines (Eds.), *Social drinking contexts* (Research Monograph No. 7) (pp. 34–53). Rockville, MD: National Institute on Alcohol Abuse and Alcoholism.

Flavin, D. K., Franklin, J. E., & Frances, R. J. (1986). The acquired immune deficiency syndrome (AIDS) and suicidal behavior in alcohol-dependent homosexual men. *American Journal of Psychiatry, 143,* 1440–1442.

Frances, R. J., Wikstrom, T., & Alcena V. (1985). Contracting AIDS as a means of committing suicide. *American Journal of Psychiatry, 142,* 1440.

Glassner, B., & Loughlin, J. (1987). *Drugs in adolescent worlds.* New York: Macmillan.

Goffman, E. (1959). The moral career of the mental patient. *Psychiatry: Journal for the Study of Interpersonal Processes, 22,* 123–135.

Goode, E. (1989). *Drugs in American society (3rd ed.).* New York: Knopf.

Greenberg, D. F. (1988). *The construction of homosexuality.* Chicago: The University of Chicago Press.

Haer, J. L. (1955). Drinking patterns and the influence of friends and family. *Quarterly Journal of Studies on Alcohol, 16,* 178–185.

Helzer, J. E., & Przybeck, T. R. (1988). The co-occurrence of alcoholism with other psychiatric disorders in the general population and its impact on treatment. *Journal of Studies on Alcohol, 49,* 219–224.

Hirschi, T. (1969). *Causes of delinquency.* Berkeley: University of California Press.

Hooker, E. (1967). The homosexual community. In J. H. Gagnon & W. Simon (Eds.), *Sexual deviance* (pp. 167–184). New York: Harper Row.

Hughes, J. A. (1979). Alienation. In G. D. Mitchell (Ed.), *A new dictionary of the social sciences* (pp. 4–6). New York: Aldine.

Humphreys, L. (1970). *Tearoom trade: Impersonal sex in public places.* Chicago: Aldine.

Icard, L., & Traunstein, D. M. (1987). Black, gay, alcoholic men: Their character and treatment. *Social Casework, 68,* 267–272.

Israelstam, S., & Lambert, S. (1984). Gay bars. *Journal of Drug Issues, 4,* 637–653.

Jackson, J. K. (1954). The adjustment of the family to the crisis of alcoholism. *Quarterly Journal of Studies on Alcohol, 15,* 562–586.

Jackson, J. K. (1962). Alcoholism and the family. In D. J. Pittman & C. R. Snyder (Eds.), *Society, culture, and drinking patterns* (pp. 472–492). Carbondale, IL: Southern Illinois University Press.

Jellinek, E. M. (1960). *The disease concept of alcoholism.* New Haven, CT: Hillhouse Press.

Jellinek, E. M. (1962). Phases of alcohol addiction. In D. J. Pittman & C. R. Snyder (Eds.), *Society, culture, and drinking patterns* (pp. 356–368). Carbondale, IL: Southern Illinois University Press.

Jones, C. C., Waskin, H., Gerety, B., Skipper, B., Hull, H. F., & Mertz, G. J. (1987). Persistence of high-risk sexual activity among homosexual men in an area of low incidence of the acquired immunodeficiency syndrome. *Sexually Transmitted Diseases, 14,* 79–82.

Joseph, J. G., Montgomery, S. B., Emmons, C-A., Kirscht, J. P., Kessler, R. C., Ostrow, D. G., Wortman, C. B., & O'Brien, K. (1987). Perceived risk of AIDS: Assessing the behavioral and psychosocial consequences in a cohort of gay men. *Journal of Applied Social Psychology, 17,* 231–250.

Kamel, G. W. L. (1983). *Downtown street hustlers: The role of dramaturgical imaging practices in the social construction of male prostitution.* Unpublished doctoral dissertation, University of California, San Diego.

Kelly, J. A., St. Lawrence, J. S., Brasfield, T. L., Lemke, A., Amidei, T., Roffman, R. E., Hood, H. V., Kilgore, H., & McNeill, C., Jr. (1990). Psychological factors that predict AIDS high-risk versus AIDS precautionary behavior. *Journal of Consulting and Clinical Psychology, 58,* 117–120.

Kelly, J. A., St. Lawrence, J. S., Brasfield, T. L., Stevenson, Y., Diaz, Y. E., & Hauth, A. C. (1990). AIDS risk behavior patterns among gay men in small southern cities. *American Journal of Public Health, 80,* 416–418.

Kingsdale, J. M. (1973). The "poor man's club": Social functions of the urban working-class saloon. *American Quarterly, 25,* 472–489.

Knight, R. P. (1937). The psychodynamics of chronic alcoholism. *Journal of Nervous and Mental Disorders, 86,* 538–548.

Kraft, D. P. (1981). Public drinking practices of college youths: Implications for prevention programs. In T. C. Harford & L. S. Gaines (Eds.), *Social drinking contexts* (Research Monograph No. 7) (pp. 54–84). Rockville, MD: National Institute on Alcohol Abuse and Alcoholism.

Kus, R. J. (1988). Alcoholism and non-acceptance of gay self: The critical link. *Journal of Homosexuality, 15*(1/2), 25–41.

Leigh, B. C. (1990). The relationship of substance use during sex to high-risk sexual behavior. *Journal of Sex Research, 27,* 199–213.

LeMasters, E. E. (1973). Social life in a working-class tavern. *Urban Life and Culture, 2,* 27–52.

Lemert, E. M. (1951). *Social pathology.* New York: McGraw-Hill.

Levine, M. P. (1979). Gay ghetto. In M. P. Levine (Ed.), *Gay men: The sociology of male homosexuality* (pp. 182–204). New York: Harper & Row.

Little, C. B. (1989). *Deviance and control: Theory, research, and social policy.* Itasca, IL: F. E. Peacock.

Lofland, L. H. (1972). Self-management in public settings: 1. *Urban Life and Culture, 1*, 93–108.

Lohrenz, L. J., Connelly, J. C., Coyne, L., & Spare, K. E. (1978). Alcohol problems in several midwestern homosexual communities. *Journal of Studies on Alcohol, 39*, 1959–1963.

Machover, S., Puzzo, F. S., Machover, K., & Plumeau, F. (1959). Clinical and objective studies of personality variables in alcoholism: 3. An objective study of homosexuality in alcoholism. *Quarterly Journal of Studies on Alcohol, 20*, 528–542.

MacIver, R. M. (1950). *The ramparts we guard.* New York: Macmillan.

Maddox, G. L. (1962). Teenage drinking in the United States. In D. J. Pittman & C. R. Snyder (Eds.), *Society, culture, and drinking patterns* (pp. 230–245). Carbondale, IL: Southern Illinois University Press.

Maddox, G. L. (1968). Role making: Negotiations in emergent drinking careers. *Social Science Quarterly, 49*, 331–349.

Martin, J. L. (1987). The impact of AIDS on gay male sexual behavior patterns in New York City. *American Journal of Public Health, 77*, 578–581.

Matza, D. (1969). *Becoming deviant.* Englewood Cliffs, NJ: Prentice-Hall.

Matza, D., & Sykes, G. (1961). Juvenile delinquency and subterranean values. *American Sociological Review, 26*, 712–719.

McCaghy, C. H. (1976). *Deviant behavior: Crime, conflict, and interest groups.* New York: Macmillan.

McCord, W., & McCord, J. (1960). *Origins of alcoholism.* Stanford, CA: Stanford University Press.

McKirnan, D. J., & Peterson, P. L. (1988). Stress, expectancies, and vulnerability to substance abuse: A test of a model among homosexual men. *Journal of Abnormal Psychology, 97*, 461–466.

McKirnan, D. J., & Peterson, P. L. (1989). Psychosocial and cultural factors in alcohol and drug abuse: An analysis of a homosexual community. *Addictive Behaviors, 14*, 555–563.

McKusick, L., Horstman, W., & Coates, T. J. (1985). AIDS and sexual behavior reported by gay men in San Francisco. *American Journal of Public Health, 75*, 493–496.

Merton, R. K. (1949). *Social theory and social structure.* Glencoe, IL: Free Press.

Miller, W. B. (1958). Lower class culture as a generating milieu of gang delinquency. *Journal of Social Issues, 14*(3), 5–19.

Mizruchi, E. H., & Perrucci, R. (1962). Norm qualities and differential effects of deviant behavior: An exploratory analysis. *American Sociological Review, 27*, 391–399.

Molgaard, C. A., Nakamura, C., Hovell, M., & Elder, J. P. (1988). Assessing alcoholism as a risk factor for acquired immunodeficiency syndrome (AIDS). *Social Science and Medicine, 27*, 1147–1152.

Mongeon, J. E., & Ziebold, T. O. (1982). Preventing alcohol abuse in the gay community: Toward a theory and a model. *Journal of Homosexuality*, 7(4), 89–99.

Nardi, P. (1982a). Alcohol treatment and the non-traditional "family" structures of gays and lesbians. *Journal of Alcohol and Drug Education, 27*, 83–89.

Nardi, P. (1982b). Alcoholism and homosexuality: A theoretical perspective. *Journal of Homosexuality, 7*(4), 9–25.

Nardi, P. (1991). Alcoholism and homosexuality: A theoretical perspective. In D. J. Pittman & H. R. White (Eds.), *Society, culture, and drinking patterns reexamined* (pp. 285–305). New Brunswick, NJ: Rutgers Center of Alcohol Studies.

National Institute on Drug Abuse. (1986). *Highlights of the 1985 national household survey on drug abuse.* Rockville, MD: National Institute on Drug Abuse.

Prout, C. T., Strongin, E. I., & White, M. A. (1950). A study of results in hospital treatment of alcoholism in males. *American Journal of Psychiatry, 107*, 14–19.

Prus, R. (1983). Drinking as activity: An interactionist analysis. *Journal of Studies on Alcohol, 44*, 460–475.

Ray, M. B. (1961). The cycle of abstinence and relapse among heroin addicts. *Social Problems, 9*, 132–140.

Read, K. E. (1980). *Other voices: The style of a male homosexual tavern.* Novato, CA: Chandler and Sharp.

Reinarman, C., & Leigh, B. C. (1987). Culture, cognition, and disinhibition: Notes on sexuality and alcohol in the age of AIDS. *Contemporary Drug Problems, 14*, 435–460.

Reitzes, D. C., & Diver, J. K. (1982). Gay bars as deviant community organizations: The management of interactions with outsiders. *Deviant Behavior, 4*, 1–18.

Riggall, R. (1923). Homosexuality and alcoholism. *Psychoanalytic Review, 10*, 157–169.

Roebuck, J., & Spray, S. L. (1967). The cocktail lounge: A study of heterosexual relations in a public organization. *American Journal of Sociology, 72*, 388–395.

Rogers, P. (1993, February 15). How many gays are there? A new debate about the numbers of homosexuals. *Newsweek*, p. 46.

Rudy, D. R. (1986). *Becoming alcoholic: Alcoholics Anonymous and the reality of alcoholism.* Carbondale, IL: Southern Illinois University Press.

Ruefli, T., Yu, O., & Barton, J. (1992a). *Bar attendance and sexual risk taking among gay men.* Buffalo, NY: AIDS Alliance of Western New York.

Ruefli, T., Yu, O., & Barton, J. (1992b). Sexual risk taking in smaller cities: The case of Buffalo, New York. *Journal of Sex Research, 29*, 95–108.

Schilit, R., Clark, W. M., & Shallenberger, E. A. (1988). Social supports and lesbian alcoholics. *Affilia*, 3(2), 27–40.

Seeman, M. (1959). On the meaning of alienation. *American Sociological Review*, 24, 783–791.

Shibutani, T. (1955). Reference groups as perspectives. *American Journal of Sociology*, 60, 562–568.

Shilts, R. (1976, February 25). Alcoholism: A look in depth at how a national menace is affecting the gay community. *Advocate*, pp. 16–19, 22–25.

Siegel, K., Mesagno, F. P., Chen, J-Y., & Christ, G. (1989). Factors distinguishing homosexual males practicing risky and safer sex. *Social Science and Medicine*, 28, 561–569.

Small, E. J., Jr., & Leach, B. (1977). Counseling homosexual alcoholics: Ten case histories. *Journal of Studies on Alcohol*, 38, 2077–2086.

Smith, S. B., & Schneider, M. A. (1981). Treatment of gays in a straight environment: Gay alcoholics, drug addicts survive a "straight inpatient milieu." In A. J. Schecter (Ed.), *Drug Dependence and Alcoholism: Vol. 2. Social and Behavioral Issues* (pp. 131–140). New York: Plenum.

Smith, T. M. (1982). Specific approaches and techniques in the treatment of gay male alcohol abusers. *Journal of Homosexuality*, 7(4), 53–69.

Stall, R. D., Coates, T. J., & Hoff, C. (1988). Behavioral risk reduction for HIV infection among gay and bisexual men: A review of results from the United States. *American Psychologist*, 43, 878–885.

Stall, R., Heurtin-Roberts, S., McKusick, L., Hoff, C., & Lang, S. W. (1990). Sexual risk for HIV transmission among singles-bar patrons in San Francisco. *Medical Anthropology Quarterly*, 4, 115–128.

Stall, R., McKusick, L., Wiley, J., Coates, T. J., & Ostrow, D. G. (1986). Alcohol and drug use during sexual activity and compliance with safe sex guidelines for AIDS: The AIDS behavioral research project. *Health Education Quarterly*, 13, 359–371.

Stall, R., & Wiley, J. (1988). A comparison of alcohol and drug use patterns of homosexual and heterosexual men: The San Francisco Men's Health Study. *Drug and Alcohol Dependence*, 22, 63–73.

Straus, R., & Bacon, S. B. (1953). *Drinking in College*. Westport, CT: Greenwood Press.

Straus, R., & Bacon, S. B. (1962). The problems of drinking in college. In D. J. Pittman & C. R. Snyder (Eds.), *Society, culture, and drinking patterns* (pp. 246–258). Carbondale, IL: Southern Illinois University Press.

Trice, H. M., & Roman, P. (1970). Delabeling, relabeling, and Alcoholics Anonymous. *Social Problems*, 17, 538–546.

Troiden, R. R. (1979). Becoming homosexual. *Psychiatry: Journal for the Study of Interpersonal Processes*, 42, 362–373.

Ullman, A. D. (1962). First drinking experience as related to age and sex. In D. J. Pittman & C. R. Snyder (Eds.), *Society, culture, and drinking patterns.* (pp. 259–266). Carbondale, IL: Southern Illinois University Press.

Wallace, R. A., & Wolf, A. (1991). *Contemporary sociological theory: Continuing the classical tradition* (3rd ed.). Englewood Cliffs, NJ: Prentice-Hall.

Warren, C. A. B. (1974). *Identity and community in the gay world.* New York: John Wiley.

Watson, D. R., & Weinberg, T. S. (1982). Interviews and the interactional construction of accounts of homosexual identity. *Social Analysis, 11,* 56–78.

Weinberg, T. S. (1978). On "doing" and "being" gay: Sexual behavior and homosexual male self-identity. *Journal of Homosexuality, 4,* 143–156.

Weinberg, T. S. (1983). *Gay men, gay selves: The social construction of homosexual identities.* New York: Irvington.

Weinberg, T. S. (1984). Biology, ideology, and the reification of developmental stages in the study of homosexual identities. *Journal of Homosexuality, 10*(3/4), 77–84.

Weinberg, T. S., & Vogler, C. C. (1990). Wives of alcoholics: Stigma management and adjustments to husband-wife interaction. *Deviant Behavior, 11,* 331–343.

Whitney, S. (1982). The ties that bind: Strategies for counseling the gay male co-alcoholic. *Journal of Homosexuality, 7*(4), 37–41.

Windle, M. (1989). High-risk behaviors for AIDS among heterosexual alcoholics: A pilot study. *Journal of Studies on Alcohol, 50,* 503–507.

Wiseman, J. P. (1970). *Stations of the lost: The treatment of skid row alcoholics.* Englewood Cliffs, NJ: Prentice-Hall.

Wiseman, J. P. (1979, August). *Sober comportment: Patterns and perspectives on alcohol addiction.* Paper presented at the meetings of the American Sociological Association, Boston, MA.

Wiseman, J. P. (1980). The "home treatment": The first steps in trying to cope with an alcoholic husband. *Family Relations, 29,* 541–549.

Yearwood, L., & Weinberg, T. S. (1979). Black organizations, gay organizations: Sociological parallels. In M. P. Levine (Ed.), *Gay men: The sociology of male homosexuality* (pp. 301–316). New York: Harper Row.

Ziebold, T. O. (1978). *Alcoholism and the gay community.* Washington, DC: Blade Communications.

Ziebold, T. O., & Mongeon, J. E. (1982). Introduction: Alcoholism and the homosexual community. *Journal of Homosexuality, 7*(4), 3–7.

Zigrang, T. A. (1982). Who should be doing what about the gay alcoholic? *Journal of Homosexuality, 7*(4), 27–35.

Index

Abraham, K., 1

Abstinence: reasons for, 84–87; and relapse cycles, 84–89; responses of others to, 84, 87–88; self-definition and, 117–22

Achilles, N., 3, 31, 34, 35, 36, 37, 42, 52, 56

Adam, B. D., 139

Adam: on being gay, 137

AIDS: and alcohol use, 45, 48, 171–72n.5; as means of committing suicide, 48; in Paradise City, 48

Aitken, P. P., 51, 170n.1

Alan: on drinking with his mother, 79; on his alcohol use, 105; on his initial feelings about drinking, 78; on his regular bar, 145; reasons for abstention of, 85

Alcena, V., 48

Alcohol and entertaining, 61–62

Alcoholic: definition of, 168n.1; labeling self as, 168n.1

Alcoholic drinks: number consumed, 79; types preferred, 79

Alcoholics: drinking patterns of, 170n.2; similarities between gay and heterosexual, 149

Alcoholism: knowledge about, 65; of parents, 79–80, 96, 97, 140–42; sequential model of, 174n.3; and sexual orientation, 90, 122–25, 156–57; of siblings, 80

Alcohol use: amount of, 93; attitudes toward, 90, 152–53; and cruising, 42–49; current, 89–93; and disinhibition, 44–46; frequency of, 92–93, 173n.7; returning to, 87–89; and sexual risk taking among gays, 45–49; and sexual risk taking among heterosexuals, 46. *See also* Drinking

Alienation: and drinking, 131–40; in gay alcoholism literature, 126–27, 147, 148; and problem drinkers, 147–48; problems of as explanation for gay drinking, 127–28; uses of concept of, 128–31

Anomy: Durkheim's description of, 129; Merton's conceptualization of, 174n.3

Art: on coming out, 95; drinking history of, 95; on reasons for abstinence, 86; on reasons for resuming drinking, 89

Bacon, S. B., 93, 169n.2, 170n.3, 173n.4

Barhopping, 32, 43; influence of friends on, 49

Bar inducements, 51–56, 172n.7

Barringer, F., 2

Barry: on being gay, 123; on depression, 114; on his attitude to-

184

Erik: on alcohol use and cruising, 45; on bar attendance, 62; on drinking at home, 61; on early feelings about drinking, 78; on father's alcoholism, 140; on his religious beliefs, 136

Ernie: on drinking, 100; drinking history of, 96

Extended families, 19–20, 150, 174n.1; and alcohol awareness, 157–58; and bars, 34–35; influence on drinking of, 70–71

Familial relations, 133–35

Family: frequency of contact with, and drinking, 134; influences on early drinking of, 79–80; residence of, and drinking, 134–35

Fenichel, O., 1

Fifield, L. H., 2, 33, 126, 127, 147, 168–69n.1

Fisher, J. C., 21, 62, 136, 144, 146, 149

Flavin, D. K., 48

Frances, R. J., 48

Frank: on bars and coming out, 38; on drinking as a habit, 89; drinking history of, 76

Franklin, J. E., 48

Friends: and bars, 49–51, 143, 144–45; and buying drinks, 81–84; and drinking, for gays, 19–21, 49–50, 145–46; and drinking, for heterosexuals, 50–51, 146, 170n.1

Gary: on being gay, 137; on depression, 138; on drinking and parties, 20; on factors in bar visitation, 21; reasons for abstinence of, 85

Gay AA, meeting of, 175n.2

Gay alcoholics: behavior of, 124, 149; drinking rationales of, 149

Gay bars: age at first attendance in, 37, 143; appeal of, 52; back rooms in, 48–49; coming out in, 37–39, 151; and drinking involvement, 143; as drinking settings, 21; factors affecting attendance in, 39–40, 170nn. 7, 8; first visits to, 38–39; frequency of attendance at, 143, 144, 151; functions of, 35–36, 37, 143; importance of, 32–37; interactions in, 40–57, 149; as late-night world, 37; leaving the, 56–57; length of time attending, 144; location of, 32, 36; making sexual contacts in, 42–49; reasons for attending, 35–36, 77; and social acceptance, 33–34, 77, 99, 150; as social centers, 33–36; stability of, 31; types of, in Paradise City, 11, 32

Gay Center, the: coming out in, 95; description of, 10

Gay couples: drinking behavior of, 60–63; and extended families, 70–71; in study, 172n.1. See also Love relationships

Gay identity: acquiring a, 18–19, 150; feelings about one's, 123, 136–37; functions of bars for, 34; and problem drinking, 137

Gay institutions, 16–17, 34, 150

Gay organizations, 16–17; and bar attendance, 151, 153; depression, 139; and drinking involvement, 139, 153; and happiness, 139; importance of, 153; membership in, 139, 151

Gay subculture: as leisure world, 36–37; participation in, 143–46, 150, 151; support of relationships by, 67, 70–71

Geographic mobility, and drinking problems, 135

Thomas S. Weinberg is a professor of sociology at Buffalo State College. He received his bachelor's and master's degrees from Rutgers University and his Ph.D. from the University of Connecticut. His research interests include deviance, addiction and alcoholism, and sexual behavior. Weinberg's prior work has appeared in *Deviant Behavior, Journal of Sex Research, Journal of Homosexuality, Journal of Drug Issues, Bulletin of the American Academy of Psychiatry and the Law,* and *Journal of Psychology & Human Sexuality*. He is the coeditor of *S and M: Studies in Sadomasochism* and the author of *Gay Men, Gay Selves: The Social Construction of Homosexual Identities.*